NOW

Overcoming Crushing Grief by Living in the Present

NOW

Overcoming Crushing Grief by Living in the Present

JACK CAIN
ANNE HATCHER BERENBERG, PH.D.

© 2001-2008 Jack Cain

Published 2009

Printed in the United States

ISBN 978-0-578-01155-4

Library of Congress Control Number 2009901102

Book cover design by
    Illumination Graphics, www.illuminationgraphics.com

Book interior design by
    Prepress Solutions, www.prepress-solutions.com

JJC Publications
1443 Scott Ave.
Winnetka, IL 60093
jack@living-in-the-now.com

The Poem on Page 5 is used with the gracious permission from
the author Tom Hawkins and Sun Magazine

When Anna was ill,
I would have seen her as the fallen bird,
injured in the road, as I hovered,
watching her struggles,
urging her to fly on broken wings.

But now she is gone,
with our marathon conversations,
her startling questions.

And I don't know
which of those two birds
I am.

Excerpt from the poem *Describe Your Grief*, Tom Hawkins
Sun Magazine, July 2008

✛

CONTENTS

✜

INTRODUCTION

Three tragic experiences in my life could have virtually destroyed me. I deliberately chose not to be destroyed. Instead I taught myself to overcome the grief that was consuming me and to bring my mind—and me—back into the land of the living. This book will tell you how to do the same.

Three people in my family died in a twenty month period, of unrelated causes. My son, Adam, committed suicide at age 27; then my wife, Lenore, died of ovarian cancer, after having had breast cancer four years previously; my daughter Stephanie died at age 34 of congestive heart failure, less than three months after the death of my wife.

There were only five of us to start with, and these battering blows left me and my daughter, Nicole, shattered. For a long time, people asked me how I survived them. I replied that I had no choice. It was either survive or jump off the bridge. I chose survival.

Because of my jangled mind, it took me some time to realize what I had really done to survive. It was no accident. I had a plan, born, I suppose, of desperation. The thing is, I didn't realize I had a plan until I was in the midst of using it. I'm telling you about it because I hope you will benefit from it as I have.

I taught myself to live in the present, the NOW, to leave the past behind and to not give currency to the feared future.

A feared future that might never happen. I needed to do this is order to simply survive.

This is a story of personal survival. Mental survival and emotional survival. And it is about hope and love. And how, in the end, I found a way to deal with the grief and the losses. It was, and still is, a voyage of self-discovery.

There's a good chance that you are reading this book for a purpose. Most likely, you didn't just *happen* to pick it up. Possibly, grief has entered your life and assaulted you like few things ever have before. Maybe you think you've suffered plenty and you would like to tone down the pain.

Well, you've come to the right place. I can help you. I *will* help you. I will tell you more about the grief-events in my life and what I did to survive them. And not just survive them but to come out the other side with a rainbow on my horizon every day. It wasn't easy for me. It won't be easy for you. But it will happen for you. I will walk you through the solution, every step of the way.

I came to *NOW* almost by chance. I was frequently living in the past, feeling sorry for myself. I was afraid of the future, worrying who might die next. Steering myself to *NOW* was a survival technique. I simply couldn't go on bouncing from emotional wall to emotional wall; I had to do something. I saw my goal quite clearly: I had to release myself from the pain of the grief of the past and from the anxiety of what might happen to me and my loved ones in the future. I had to learn to be—to live—in the present only. Following this path, I came to *NOW*.

And so I made myself experience it. Every day, every chance I got. Every time I went back or forward, I pulled myself once again to the center. Each time, I realized that I didn't have to keep on feeling this grief day after day. I needed to be present in the grief for about a year, but after that time I realized I needed to live, not just survive. I had to move on with my life, somehow. And I let *NOW* come into my life.

What exactly do I mean by living in the *NOW*? It is living this present moment and being present in this moment. It means valuing today for the only true reality. The past is over and your fears for the future might never happen.

Living in the NOW means choosing not to dredge up every negative thing in the past that went wrong or that caused your grief, whether you think you were involved in the cause of this grief or not. Living in the *NOW* also means not living in the negative future. Worrying, for example, who will make all the decisions now that your spouse has died.

The obvious alternative to either the past or the future is to choose a middle path. If it's neither, it must be *Now*. The word deserves that capital letter. It should really be called the Holy Now, but the religious connotation steers me back to the elegant simplicity of the single word. Once you have *chosen* to leave the negative past and the fearful future you will feel like Dorothy, seeing the Land of Oz, the Emerald City, for the first time. The land of the present contains all the positive aspects of your life as it is now and allows you to live by appreciating all that you already have that is wonderful.

I didn't invent the *NOW*. I did discover how it can be a saving grace, returning one from a land of deep grief to this land of the living. Although I was able to enter this right state of mind, at first it was more like visiting it, rather than living in it. I wasn't fully immersed. Not surprising. You need to be doing this by experiencing it. I hadn't yet experienced it enough. It was all too new.

NOW is learned by doing. It is *experienced* by doing. Think of this: you get up in the morning and then, out of nowhere, while reading the newspaper for example, thoughts come crashing through your peaceful day. Thoughts that drag you back into the past. Or thoughts that threaten you with the dreadful future that lives only in the dark recesses of your mind.

And right then and there you say Stop! Stop the pain of the past and fear of the future! I am here now in the present and I will not – repeat, not – be governed any longer by these forces. I am going to move on with my life and savor every small bit of good that comes my way. And I am going to train myself to look for those morsels in my everyday life. Because they are there for the finding.

And every time the past or future intrudes when uninvited, I will say the same. Stop!

I developed a practice of living in the positive present, not allowing myself to dwell in past pains or future worries, as a way to overcome grief and loss. Some time after I started writing this book of practical insight and inspiration, another book with Now in the title was published: *The Power of Now*, by Eckhart Tolle. Mr. Tolle sets out a philosophy dealing with spirituality and living in the present. His valuable book is based on possibilities, whereas mine is based on the real life experience of overcoming crushing grief. I aim to give you guideposts and ways to apply living in the NOW to everyday life. It can easily be used together with Mr. Tolle's book if his spiritually oriented insights resonate with you, or my book can stand alone.

Joan Didion, in her book *The Year of Magical Thinking*, details, with great clarity her reaction to grief. Grief that resulted from the death of her husband: sudden, sharp and shocking. When you finish reading it, you will feel great empathy for her, wondering how someone survives such loss. Living in the NOW helps to answer this question.

My insights also give a different perspective to those shown in Elisabeth Kübler Ross's famous book, *On Death And Dying*. She saw grief as a linear process, going from one to the next in her famous Five Stages of Grieving. I don't see it this way; to me grief is a circular or more accurately, spiral process. As you are wandering in the wilderness, each time you enter it you also reenter it. It is usually different than the last time and there are no road signs to lead you. Yet, as you revisit areas you've seen before, you realize you're looking at them from slightly vantage points and you are slowly progressing.

Mindfulness is a Buddhist concept. It also happens to be a large part of what I advocate. It means dropping the past and the future and living solely in the present. It would be hard to find more complete spirituality. My sort of spirituality includes Crowding Out the Negatives. The Buddhist spiritual practice of mindfulness has important commonalities with what I am suggesting. Mindfulness means focusing your full attention on the moment, being fully present and fully aware of what you are experiencing. For example, if you are eating rice, your full attention should be on the experience of eating rice – its texture, flavor, temperature, etc. I see this kind of attention to the present moment as a way of crowding out the negatives. I show how we can fill our minds with positives, leaving no room for negative thinking. We will just have the desire to pay attention to the *NOW*.

Scott Peck begins his book *The Road Less Traveled*, with these words: "Life is difficult," which, he points out, means there are no easy answers. Faced with severe loss we are most likely to feel we cannot carry on. As time goes by, the memory lingers but gradually the pain lessens until one day we are able to cope with something we never expected to cope with. At that point we become capable of leaving the past and ignoring the future. We learn to live in the present moment and to treasure all that still remains in our lives after the loss. We will allow the unneeded scales to drop away and to teach ourselves that there is something to be learned, even from tragedy.

This tragedy might come from something sudden such as the death of a spouse from a heart attack; or it might be a death from a prolonged illness, such as cancer or it might come from other losses. All of these types of grief will be made more easily sustainable once you have learned to live in the *NOW*.

As was demonstrated so forcefully in my own family, age is not a determinant as to how long you will live, nor is your position in the family. I was the oldest and have already outlived my wife and two children. You might die at 30 as well as 90. Living in this moment removes age from the equation.

There are two different types of *NOW*. One is simply a measurement of a sliver of time; the other requires choosing to live the best possible *NOW* we can. But *sliver* is putting too fine a point on it. The sliver might be the few seconds that surround you at any given moment, or it might be the hour you're living in right now; it might be all of today. One thing is for certain: *NOW* can only be contained in this day, today, at the most. Not yesterday. Not tomorrow.

The other type of *NOW* realizes that 'choosing' is the operative word, and this is my path: I consistently turned 'right' to find if there was anything positive in a given situation and then did what I could to possibly improve it, rather than turning 'left' and inviting the quicksand of the negative.

Most of us hold onto the past and beat up on ourselves for perceived errors we've made. Some from opportunities missed by lack of decision. Or, decisions that have been made, some unfortunate and others almost disastrous.

It isn't enough to just find the *NOW* and be in it. You must decide on the *best NOW* for the maximum mental and emotional well-being.

A friend, who appears to be about 60, told me in another context that she had more years behind her than in front of her. If she followed the *NOW*, there would be no years behind her nor any in front of her. There would just be today, not carrying any of the baggage of yesterday or tomorrow. How common it is for someone to remark that the years seem to be flying by and that this seems to increase as one gets older. How common and how unnecessary.

Throughout this book I have made commentaries at the end of some chapters with references to the *NOW*. If you are able to absorb this concept into your being, you will be able to say, as I do, that you can't believe how lucky you are, in spite of any misfortunes you might have had, which after all, are in the past, not in the *NOW*.

Imagine giving yourself this present: that the next time someone asks how old you are, you reply, "I don't have, or need, birthdays any more. I live in the *NOW*!" And you don't *simply reply*, you mean it.

From birth we have learned to wallow in the negative past and constantly ask ourselves: *Why me?* The twin sibling to this is fearing the future, and all the negatives it might hold. Might. We have to get rid of these two, but how?

In order to learn the *NOW*, it must be practiced every day. First, of course, is simply the *learning* practice: finding out how to do it. Then comes the other type of practice: it is that which we already know but need to keep using, to keep it polished and usable. I will give you specific examples of living in the *NOW* as we go along, together with comments about how you can apply these examples to your own life.

I have created Ten Steps that are used to achieve this survival. They evolved from a process I went thru to retain my grip on reality. I was grasping for some scaffolding to hang on to. Later, as I was developing this book, I realized that everyone else would also be in the same state I was. They would need beacons to show them the way. As I was living the process I didn't have the advantage of having these Steps as my virtual *Sherpas* that showed me the way and carried my burden. As I went along they came to me because I needed them.

Using these Steps, which comprise the last chapter of this book, will guide you on your path back to mental balance. The Steps don't need to be followed in a linear way, other than Step #1. You can go, for instance from #7 back to #3 and then forward again to #6. It becomes the choice of the reader to decide which Step fits your life and your stage of grief at any particular moment.

However . . . . and this is very important . . . . if you feel a need to go immediately to the Ten Steps, by all means do so. You can always go back to the beginning of the book when you are ready.

These Steps are followed by Reinforcements which will allow you to make practical use of the information in that Step. In essence, Reinforcements are examples as to how you might imagine applying the Step to *your* life.

Anne Hatcher Berenberg, Ph.D. co-authored the commentary sections at the ends of chapters and the Ten Steps, taking primary responsibility for the Reinforcements which conclude each step. Anne has a B.A. in Social Relations from Harvard University, an M.A. in Psychology from Boston University, and a Ph.D. in Clinical Psychology from the City University of New York. Her background and experience as a clinical psychologist, currently in private practice, formerly as Director of Psychology at the Josselyn Center for Mental Health in Northfield, Illinois, as well as her personal experience of having been widowed, has given the book an important added dimension.

Lest there be some confusion, let me say that living in the *NOW* doesn't mean we have forgotten the past. Perhaps, for instance, we acknowledge that our mother has died. We *know* that she has died but after a significant length of time devoted to grieving, we have chosen not to become mired in grief. We move on and live in the present only. But at the same time, we have reserved a place in our lives for remembrance. We will continue to love and remember our loved one, while recognizing that our life must go on.

Similarly, imagine that we are planning a phenomenal party five months down the road and can't wait for it to be here; or, on the negative side, we are planning to have surgery in two weeks and dread the event. In both cases, we don't need to drive ourselves wild with anticipation for the former or crazy with fear for the latter. We are living in the *NOW*. There is such a thing as trying to over-control. Both will happen when they happen, in the way they should happen. Between now and then there need be only peace of mind.

It goes without saying, of course, that we can and should make plans for the future. But why would you want or need to make your mind churn in the process?

Life, as we know, is a series of choices. Some are mundane: shall I go to a movie tonight or stay home? Some are potentially life-threatening: shall I have the surgery or just chance otherwise? Both are future tense, even if the future is three minutes from now.

But there are other kinds of choices, other kinds of forks in the road: these involve ongoing decisions, which are now, not in the future, about how we choose to accommodate ourselves to loss, such as that of a loved one.

Does this sound like something you do: Feeling sorry for yourself? How about getting stuck in the past? Well, that's the most normal thing I can think of. And also the most normal thing that's really dragging you down. Preventing you from living again. But you don't have to feel that way, because you have a choice. And why would you want to keep feeling that way when you can choose not to? When I discovered that I had a choice I started digging myself out of that pit and began crawling back up to the land of the living.

I want to help you do the same thing. The only thing required is that you let yourself learn it. I am so convinced that you can that sometimes I feel like an evangelist. Not for a religion but for you and your mental health. No matter what you've gone through and are still going through, help is coming. The help is the *NOW*. You're suffering from grief and there is a way to lessen it. I know the way and I want to share it with you.

Living in the *NOW* helped me through my grief by letting me pull myself away from the pain of the past and into the present. Once I accomplished this, I learned to look at the negative future I was at times imagining and taught myself that I was doing just that: imagining it. It hadn't happened yet. Why would I choose to live there?

After your loss, will you be crushed by it or instead grieve through the loss and then slowly but surely adjust and move on? Such choices are exactly that: choices. We can choose to crumble under the weight of the loss or learn that we can recover from it, no matter how severe.

Every day, almost every hour of every day at first, we need to make these life-giving decisions in order to preserve our lives. Not our physical lives but the life of our core, our being.

I was fortunate to learn, after her death, that Lenore had kept a journal. I think she did it to keep track of her feelings as she started on a journey thru this strange and dangerous new country. It was exactly the same as tapping into someone else's mind. From time to time I have quoted short passages from her journal so that you can get some idea of both our thought processes, as we lived them. But I chose not to include any larger sections in order to have the main story flow more smoothly. However, for those interested in reading the journal in its entirety I have added it to the last part of this book as Appendix A.

❖

When you turn the page, you will join me on the journey I took, however involuntarily. As I said, three people in my family died in a twenty month period. It was tragic, but I survived it. I'll tell you how. And by the end of the book, I promise to show you how you can also.

But before I can tell you how I overcame this crushing grief, I need to tell you the events that led up to their deaths.

And before I can tell you about their deaths, I need to tell you about their lives. Come with me and reenter their world that was. In the calm before my storm, in early 1993 there was not yet disease, death nor pain. Especially, there was not yet grief.

By the end of that year, the five dynamics that were our lives had converged.

✦
THE FAMILY

MY WIFE, LENORE

L enore's Jewish parents were born in Chicago; their ances-
tors lived in Lithuania and Ukraine. Her parents divorced
when she was quite young, and she and her siblings lived
with their mother. Her father was not often around, making
her mother quite bitter; the bitterness of the mother was possibly why her father was rarely around. Her mother started a
business which grew over the years. Initially, Lenore was not
in it, but after the death of her mother, she became involved
and rose to vice-president. This was a strong turnaround for
someone who was never before in business. She became a new
someone who was then heavily immersed and liked it. It gave
her a feeling of esteem and self-worth.

In spite of this, Lenore was a lioness first and a business
woman second. Above all else, she regarded her role to be the
chief protector and advocate of her children, especially Stephanie who had Down Syndrome.

Lenore's weakness with the children was that she was not
good at saying *no*. She used me for that purpose. Her difficulty
saying *no* was a problem sometimes with Adam, who pushed
beyond the limits of acceptable behavior. He always came
to Lenore when he wanted something because he knew she
would cave.

Lenore was a good person. You could count on her. If she said she would do something, she did it. She also knew that she could count on me and I would do exactly what I said I would do.

She had a narrow range of interests—her children and shopping—while I had a very wide range. This was never a conflict.

She did not discourage me from pursuing my interests–she found them interesting but didn't want to participate in any of them. I was proud of her devotion as a mother, and I was happy for her to find pleasure in shopping.

I had not minded that Lenore had been dependent on me, nor had I regarded her as weak for needing me as a pillar. It was simply a description of what was.

But when she was ready to become stronger and more independent around 1990, I encouraged her striking out on her own. She started working in her family's temporary services company, becoming head of one of the divisions. We were both happy about her success.

MY DAUGHTER STEPHANIE

Stephanie was born with Down Syndrome. In the weeks following, it became apparent that she was cyanotic. Her finger tips and the ends of her toes were a shade of blue. Talking to an eminent heart specialist we learned that she had been born with a hole, possibly two, in the septum in her heart. This is the vertical divider in the heart and the holes meant that the oxygenated blood was mixing with the blood that needed to go to the lungs to receive more oxygen. In effect, her body was being deprived of oxygen. We were told by this cardiologist that she could not live to be a year old. We were told the same thing 15 years later by another expert. But, to our great joy, she just kept on living.

Because she was so vulnerable and needed someone to do or give her what she wanted, Stephanie learned to be quite manipulative. She was a first-class, top of the line psychologist, however transparent, who knew how to bend your will to hers. Let me give you an example: she knew that you knew that she had a bad heart. Instead of going upstairs to get something she wanted, she would put on her 'poor me' face and get someone to go up and get it for her. Another: In a restaurant, Lenore restricted the volume of food Stephanie could consume and would portion off the parts she could eat and those she could not. Stephanie would eat at a fantastically slow pace, such that a person would get bored and distracted and stop paying attention. She would eat the assigned section and then little by little pick away at the forbidden zone. By the time your attention finally returned, you found that most of her plate was clean.

By 1992, Stephanie had been living at Riverside for six years. This was a community for young adults with mental retardation, where she was one of the brightest, most social members. She was making her own life, feeling some independence, having friends. She was happy, friendly, and charming, and made others happy to be with her.

Everything was fine, except that she had a heart problem that was never a problem. It was limiting because she tired easily, but never a problem.

MY DAUGHTER NICOLE

Nicole was born two years and two days after Stephanie, but because Stephanie was so short, they looked to be the same age for the first few years. Nicole was easily the smartest of the three. She did extremely well in school. This did not come automatically for her. Because she had to work for her grades, I was prouder of her than I would have been if she had had a photographic memory. After graduating from the University of Illinois, she returned to school to get a second Bachelor's in Nursing.

In 1992, Nicole was cruising along with her life and everything was fine. She was living on her own, getting a master's degree in nursing, and working.

Lenore, Nicole, and Stephanie were each coming into their own, in their very different ways.

I was happy with my relationship with each of them. I was the rock from which Lenore was launching. Lenore was Stephanie's rock. Lenore and I as a unit were a solid base for Nicole.

MY SON, ADAM

The background story was Adam. From 1988 onward, negative things were going on with him. He was troubled and troubling. What was apparent were drugs and alcohol, but there was more to it than that. Although he was bright and creative, his image of himself was negative. He had problems with anger and with self-control. He couldn't accept anyone else's authority, which led to problems in school. He wasn't on a downhill trajectory; it was continuous, steady trouble. Adam attempted to deal with his feeling of low self-esteem by weight lifting and developing his body, but it didn't really help. I felt it was my responsibility to involve myself in his life. Helping him to live a satisfying life free from alcohol and drugs was a battle I was determined to win; all I really wanted him to do was to join me in this.

Lenore's and my frustration on these subjects was complete. As much as we tried, the fact is we simply didn't know what to do that really worked. We tried many avenues, mostly with professional advice, but always felt like we were not very good at what we did. The fact that our intentions were marvelous didn't cut it when we compared intentions with results. One thing that was often suggested to us and that we invariably tried was to make a contract with Adam. He wanted something from us, such as a place to live where you could also eat. In return, we had a signed contract that he would agree to and then the three of us signed. We weren't naïve enough to think this was reality based. Instead, we felt we were amateurs dealing with a professional from the C.I.A. He never intended to keep his end of the bargain, long range. We would make the contract, Adam would stick to it for a week or so, and then go right back to his own habits. We were too chicken in the end to do tough love and make him leave.

We lost every time.

He never won.

When he was about 25 he joined the Mormon Church. In spite of our reservations as to some of their beliefs, their life style as it involved Adam was extremely appealing: they are against drugs, alcohol and pre-marital sex. It was too late for the last, but the first two were more than we could have hoped for. When he joined the church he did so with an almost evangelical fervor, savoring the idea that he had to give up his previous life style. In the manner frequently common among converts of any faith, he became more Mormon than the Mormons, giving up both alcohol and drugs and relishing his role in becoming pious.

MINOR MEDICAL ISSUES

In Nov. 1992, I went to my internist for a routine physical. The doctor found that I had a slightly elevated PSA, which could be an indicator of prostate cancer. In itself, this means nothing; it happens often. The next step is to follow-up with a biopsy to check out the prostate. I couldn't follow up right away because of a long planned trip to India with Adam.

The father-son India trip was a marvelous adventure. Adam's wide range of interests and his willingness to do things melded well with mine. We had a lot of fun together, although there were moments when his poor judgment worried me, such as when he wandered off alone our first night in New Delhi, along unknown city streets. Knowing his poor sense of direction, I was frantic when it took him hours to return, and furious when he returned.

In January, 1993 Lenore had a benign tumor removed from her right breast. We both were glad that was all it was and that it was over with.

At that point, although Lenore had had some minor medical issues, nothing major had ever happened.

I had had zero, nothing minor or major. Just a hint of some potential problem.

Life was going along.

✚

JUST AS THINGS
ARE GOING WELL

THE PHONE RINGS

On that Sunday in February I'm at home with Lenore having a nice time doing nothing. Her breast surgery is now a few days behind and the pain is virtually gone; or if not gone, the pain killers smother it. A pleasant Sunday, with Lenore saying that 'that damned football season is behind us and Jack has returned to the land of the living'. She doesn't even know how many games I would watch in one day because she goes shopping with her friend Rosemary. She has her own kind of fun.

Adam is in school in New Mexico studying God-knows-what and Stephanie is at Riverside. Nicole has completed her nurse's training and is working at Columbus Hospital. My world is under control.

With Lenore, we're lucky that the lump turned out to be benign, but luckier still that the doctor had caught it early or who knows what it might have turned into.

I, on the other hand, have just been diagnosed with prostate cancer, but again we luck out. It is a very new growth and apparently manageable. Being big on mind/body connection, I have read Bernie Siegel's book, *Love, Medicine, and Miracles* some years ago and came away thinking that if I ever got cancer I would beat it.

The phone rings and when I answer it, I'm smiling at first. Then I stop.

It begins as just another ordinary day with ordinary events, ordinary talk and ordinary people. But it will become one of a series of days that start like any other, but end quite differently. You can get up in the morning expecting nothing but the banal sameness of most of the days that preceded it. And then, as when watching an airplane hit a Twin Tower, you wonder what the hell just happened. Cognitive dissonance takes over the mind and you need a little time to release the cobwebs and adjust to what has just become reality. From that moment onward, it will define you and will have become your past.

The call is from Dr. Brill who had just removed a benign tumor from one of Lenore's breasts a few days before. I am smiling because I think it is nice that he is personally following up on her surgery. The strangeness that such a call came on a Sunday doesn't immediately occur to me. After a few minutes of conversation I stop smiling. This was to become a life-changing phone call.

He wants us to come in first thing the next morning for a discussion, without being too specific. I don't like the sound of it but don't want to infect Lenore with my instinct, and so default to my face of unconcern before hanging up the phone. She presses me for more information, but it is all I have. She doesn't like the sound of it. I do my job and tell her she was crazy to worry over something that hasn't happened, that I think nothing of it and so why should she?

Without realizing it at that moment, I was trying to draw her away from fear of the future and to pull her back into the realm of the present. There was no *past* to frame the fear but the phobic near future is available for worry if we – more specifically I – let it. Granted, the potential problem has to do with Lenore's body, not mine. But there was little separation of the mind between the two. I was no less worried about her than me.

It doesn't help that she and I have virtually zero knowledge of cancer, particularly possible breast cancer and its implications. To us as to the average person, it smacks of a death sentence. At the very least, disfiguration. Lenore has undergone surgery to remove a benign tumor in her breast. Now being called in to the surgeon's office on short notice takes away the concept of *benign* and forces us into the potential of possibly *malignant*. A harsh word that is not be spoken aloud unless you absolutely cannot possibly avoid it.

It was like being stalked by a tiger. You don't see the tiger but you do see his shadow.

I read worry on Lenore's face.

She went from a previous attitude of, 'I want to be independent. I want to run my own life. I make my own money and I spend my own money.' to 'You take over.' Both of these stances were agreeable to both of us, in their own time.

But the concept of 'we' has to be there. If Lenore thinks I alone am going to handle it, she will feel helpless. She must feel like a partner, not a victim.

The next day we will go to the doctor. Our quest is to find out what's going on: What are we doing there? Once we find out what is going on, we can think about what are we going to do about it and why. I take it on as my battle. I am certainly in control, but Lenore is not excluded.

I am establishing a plan to make the unknown known. I am telling her what *we* are going to do.

I address her obvious concern by saying we don't know anything. We haven't even talked to the doctor as yet. First we'll find out what's going on. Then we'll handle it.

I think of Anna Quindlen's book *A Short Guide to a Happy Life*. She talks about 'before' and 'after' a significant event in one's life. Each event is different, of course, but all are defined by the same sense of 'before' and 'after', measuring how life has divided thereafter along the fault lines of these two words and their meaning to us.

I can't believe this might be happening. I've always had a sort of 'savior' complex, ready to be there if and when someone has a problem, because in my mind I'm tougher than they are. But I know better than anyone that I'm not tough. It's my personal façade, my own shell to keep away the outer world and not let others see my weaknesses. The penalty is having no one to turn to in times of trouble because then I'd have to admit I'm human like everyone else. And now it's catching up with me. I'm scared to death after the phone call that something terrible is happening to Lenore. And I'm afraid that something terrible is going to happen to me and my prostate. But there's no way in hell that I'm going to open the door and let someone into my dark room where my thoughts reside.

I wish that I had a better idea how to pray. It's lonely in here.

THE SURGEON

We see the surgeon, Dr. Brill, the next day. The waiting room is small and there are three other people ahead of us. One is looking off in the middle distance and presumably has his composure under tight control; the second is fidgeting in her chair and looking decidedly uncomfortable being there; the third is quietly sniffling into her Kleenex, oblivious to the rest of us. I try to imagine from how they look as to the reason they are there; possibly they are doing the same about us.

Lenore's anticipation is as bad as you can imagine. I am as concerned as she is but in the unfortunate position of needing to pretend I'm not. Essentially we see the doctor and this is what we learn: he explained that 99% of the time when he comes up against a tumor such as he removed just days ago, he can tell by looking at it that it is benign. This was the case here, except that buried in the middle of the 'benign' tumor was a small malignancy. It surfaced only with the biopsy. Luckily, it was young and hadn't had time to progress. The odds were on our side.

And so we do what one does when there is no choice. We schedule a second surgery, eight days after the first.

I make it sound like I had the situation and myself well under control. No such thing. I am a nervous wreck. Fear of the unknown; thoughts that we are experiencing a total betrayal. Not by the doctor but by life.

In order for you, in your own life, to get a feeling for what just happened to us, imagine this: you have no mortgage on your house; it is fully paid off. One day, you get a letter in the mail that says you made a mistake; it isn't paid off. Furthermore, you haven't been making payments on this balance and the mortgage company is starting foreclosure proceedings. You almost fall out of your chair. You are frantic and don't know who to call. This has to be some mistake. You had a contract and you did what you were supposed to. What are you going to do? The next day, the problem is solved but meanwhile you have been thru 24 hours of hell.

This is similar to how we feel that day. We had a contract of sorts. This was a benign tumor. We needed to go thru the experience of having it surgically removed. And so we did. We kept our end of the bargain. That was all supposed to be behind us. And now to be told that there is some mistake. It isn't benign. Maybe it isn't life that betrays us; maybe it is Lenore's body. In any case, we are stuck holding the bag. More surgery and no choice in the matter. To make matters worse, I feel a need to tell Lenore that it is no big deal; she'll have a general anesthetic and when she wakes up all will be well. I wish that I could believe it.

This was part of Lenore's first journal entry, describing our visit to the doctor after his Sunday phone call:

> *I spent what seemed like a 12 hour night in sleepless, mental agony, waiting for the daytime to come and having arrived, wanting to be elsewhere. I'm scared to death; I'm sure Jack is too but I can't afford to care. It's taking all that I have, to worry about me and I can't spread myself past that. It just isn't fair, is it? I went through all this before, just days ago, afraid of the surgery, afraid that I might have cancer and then learning that I don't. But life doesn't let up. Won't let me be. I've paid my dues and now I was called back to see the doctor. For what?*

I don't suppose I can accurately describe to anyone just how I felt that next day. As to what I thought or didn't think. Or what was going through my mind. And why I blanked out when the doctor was talking.

I start to reconnect a little later with these words: "Sorry but . . . .more surgery." He doesn't look as regretful as I want him to. "We need to take out some more in the circumference around it. Sort of like a doughnut."

"What happens next? After the surgery?" I say.

"First we'll do radiation, then chemo. Actually, further down the line, they'll overlap. The radiation will be once a day . . .takes about five minutes . . for about six weeks and maybe nine rounds of chemo, more or less. But these are details we'll leave to the experts. I'll give you the names of three radiation oncologists and three medical oncologists."

Our lives are, from that day forward, focused on a disease. And the hope that we will find a way to cure it.

This is a perfect example of the need for an advocate to accompany you either to a doctor's visit or to a hospital, something I have long advised. If I had not been there, Lenore might have heard nothing, or at least processed nothing.

Medical personnel, and medical surroundings, can be intimidating, even though this isn't the intention. This need isn't limited to people who are feeling vulnerable. When we are faced with bad news, or simply a patient in a hospital, there are things we just don't hear, and in any case we are less able to make critical judgments at such times and absolutely need someone to be our advocate. To speak for us when we cannot.

After writing this, I had an endoscopy, which requires a sort of twilight sleep during the procedure. After returning to real life, I was hearing but not really comprehending, not processing information, as I mentioned above. Luckily, I had my fiancée, Anne, with me. She was able to speak lucidly for me at that time, and just as importantly, tell me what happened afterward. Happily, the results were negative, but if they had been positive, I can easily imagine that I would have blanked out on certain portions of the conversation with the doctor.

SECOND SURGERY

And here we are, preparing for surgery, eight days after the first. My feeling is one of disbelief and weirdness that we're here again. Same hospital, same floor, same nurses, same doctor. I know it's true, but I can't believe this.

It will be hard to feel relief after the surgery. Do I believe this one? I believed the first one; they were wrong then. Are they wrong now?

These are more of Lenore's thoughts, from her journal:

That night after Jack left, I lay there in my room and started thinking. Thinking at night was both a blessing and a curse. It's a blessing because I had the time to think without interruption from the nurse or from Jack or from anyone else. But it's also a curse because the worst time to think negative thoughts is late night alone in hospital

I am never afraid of death itself. I am afraid of suffering. I am afraid of loss of control. But the fear of death did consume me when I thought of separation from my family: my daughters, my son, and Jack. And most of all it is the fear of never being able to see my first grandchild. I never knew when a grandchild might come along, but then I never knew when I might die either. As if this weren't enough, I had radiation and chemo waiting in the background. I still didn't know what to expect from either of these.

Fear of the unknown is the common thread throughout. This fear can become larger than any possible reality. Knowing that the surgery was behind her was in itself a comfort to Lenore.

Obviously, fear of the unknown is entirely a fear of the future.

Talking to a nurse who recently had breast cancer did much to mollify the unknown of chemo and radiation.

And the doctor, speaking to her in an honest, forthright manner, made her feel, at the very least, that no one was keeping anything from her.

Coping becomes both possible and easier when you are presented with a frank assessment of your disease and the prognosis, combined with talking to someone, such as the nurse, who had already been there.

MORE DOCTORS—THIS TIME FOR JACK

Following my return from India late in January, I had a repeat PSA *(prostatic specific antigens)*, the blood test which can be an early indication of prostate cancer. I was told that the reading in itself was not a terrible number, but it was high enough that more biopsies were required. I have a hard time that Monday with Lenore, sitting in Dr. Brill's waiting room, trying to deal with what passes for reality, not knowing if her tumor is really benign and at the same time waiting for the results of my biopsy.

Four days later, after the results of the biopsy are known, Dr. Redman calls to give me the news. He starts out by saying that 11 of the 12 areas of biopsy are clean. I immediately wince at the implications for the last one. Who cares about the 11 good ones? He then says that the 12th shows that there is a very small cancer in that section that of course, has to be dealt with. I instantly get a sinking feeling; but then, the next day I fixate on the idea that I am very lucky to have caught the cancer at such an early stage and therefore have all options open to me. In a former life I must have been a detective or a researcher, because my instinct is immediately to start delving into all the avenues of possibilities. I contact Lenore's brother because I know he has an acquaintance who had had prostate cancer. I also begin talking to urologists recommended by Dr. Redman.

I have entered a world of fear. The unknown has come at me, and I can't stop processing the chain of thoughts that have captured me. I know I have business stress; I had been worrying that I might actually have prostate cancer, and now I am terrified because Lenore has breast cancer. It is too much. There are three possible problems; I can't imagine that two have overtaken me. And the idea that all three are possible isn't reasonable. At least not in this abbreviated time frame.

I feel that it is almost a personal insult that I could have a diagnosis of prostate cancer, a disease. Disbelief that this could happen to me. This happens to other people. It does not happen to me.

My second reaction is disbelief that this is happening only two weeks after Lenore's diagnosis.

In a two week period, we go from having no significant medical problems, to both of us being diagnosed with cancer. It is like a one-two punch. Pow! Your head goes this way; Pow! Your head goes that way. Quite startling.

I am not totally shocked that Lenore has breast cancer, I suppose because she is a smoker and I am obnoxiously neurotic on the subject.

But I am surprised by my own diagnosis.

It becomes easier for me to cope because my diagnosis is straight forward, both as to its degree and its identification, making research as to the types of therapy available potentially more available.

Once again, I feel pulled to find out all about it. I will get all the information and I will beat this thing. The subterranean thing going on is: It's very dangerous but I don't know anything about it.

The fear was fear of the unknown. I am determined to find out about it so I could change it from unknown to known. I move into the 'Do something about it mode' on two fronts simultaneously–Lenore's and mine, reactions that are typical of my personality. If something bad comes along, I don't tend to go to pieces.

I'm most comfortable when I'm in control, even if it doesn't seem like I can control it, like cancer. With cancer, it's a fiction to say you can.

The difference is, to the degree I could control the situation, I controlled it. Control what you can; let go of what you cannot.

If an event arises that both requires someone to take charge and someone who wants me to, I'm just fine with that. If somebody says to me, 'Boy, I'm scared. I don't know what to do here. I wish you'd take over. That's all I need and away I go. That's what happened with Lenore.

These were scary days, filled with fear of what we didn't know and feelings that there was very little we had control over. The doctors were wonderful, but they were operating only on tools at their disposal and those tools were flawed. One day we will look back on this era and think of therapies such as chemo the way we presently look at 17th Century blood letting. Our doctors are doing a wonderful job with what they've got, but what they've got is still primitive. The breakthroughs in ant-angiogenesis,—depriving the cancer cells of blood supply and either killing them off or preventing new ones from growing – or in cell research, are not yet here. Both theories were thought to be the possible solution to the puzzle: what will stop the growth of cancer cells? Better yet, what will prevent the cells from starting to grow in the first place? But after promising starts, neither worked. Many researchers then started looking in other directions. I personally believe that the answer will one day lie in one of these two, maybe not alone, but possibly in combination with other agents.

Even though we could not control our situation, we could and did control how we approached it. We made it our choice to investigate the courses of treatment open to us and then to choose which choice to follow. It became a source of power to us, however small; we who previously thought we had no power in such situations. There is one thing that will almost guarantee a downward slide, both mentally and physically, and that is to feel there is no hope and that we must place our lives, unquestioningly, in the hands of experts.

We then cross a threshold and become patients. Patients, in the sense of people who are passive and have less hope and even less control over their treatment. Instead, we need to be partners with our health care professionals in order to join together in finding a way past our disease.

As we went forward with our doctors, it was as empowered partners who were learning as we went. The pleasant surprise was that the doctors were so willing to teach. It was a lesson not to be afraid to ask questions and to not accept treatments and even diagnoses as if they were commandments.

We found that most doctors we came in contact with seemed more comfortable with partners rather than patients. They apparently feel that they can more intelligently discuss the ramifications of a disease with someone who is intimately involved in his or her recovery. As I said, many people sometimes regard them as god-like; doctors don't necessarily share this view.

✚

DIFFICULTIES INCREASE

"MY APPREHENSION . . . WAS UNNECESSARY"

Excerpt from Lenore's journal:

> *The whole radiation thing sounded logical to me, and Jack and I agreed to move forward with it. My apprehension, it turned out, was unnecessary.*
>
> *After I started the radiation therapy we felt it would be a good idea to talk to the man who would be directing my next area of treatment, the chemotherapy. I had always said for years that if I ever got cancer I would never go through chemo. But now that I was faced with the decision, I realized that I wasn't so sure and that I was reserving judgment until I talked to the doctor.*

I wasn't totally aware of Lenore's fear because I knew she was counting on me to solve the problem. When I read later that she had this fear, and it was something I didn't know, I wasn't surprised. I would have been more surprised about somebody who had a potentially life-threatening disease and wasn't afraid.

Anything Lenore wanted to find out, she usually found out by way of me. This was the way she dealt with her fear of the unknown.

With Lenore, I took the stance: The problem is here, we need to solve it. Even though I kept saying 'we', I always realized it was 'I'. I had no doubt it would be solved. Yet, in spite of that strong statement, I was afraid I was wrong. I knew nothing about breast cancer and prognosis in general and as it applied to her. I was afraid she could die from it because lots of people do.

This was almost totally this fear of the unknown. I felt if I could identify the extent of the problem, I and we could beat it.

The responsibility I felt for Lenore's trust in me was almost crushing. While I felt absolutely that we were on the right path, the 'absolutely' part was very thin. I felt doubts coming at me from every side.

As I read Lenore's thoughts years after she wrote them, I am filled with gratitude that she did an uncharacteristic thing: putting her thoughts down on paper. I also get choked with emotion, being able to look into her feelings and fears as she went through this ordeal. She always had me at her side, but in many ways when we are forced to confront the difficult parts of life, we travel it alone. We are left with our own thoughts in the middle of the night, staring at the ceiling in a mostly darkened room. The fear of the future that we experience at times such as these is tamed, not by our spouse or partner, but by ourselves once we have learned to remain in the present. This ability to live always in the present might not save our lives in the usual sense, but it will save the quality of our lives and our ability to retain our sanity when the pressure of life's reversals threatens to crush us.

It is more than easy to ignore this. To imagine the horrible things that might await us down the road. To fixate on the negatives that we have heard about and start to bring into our thought patterns. But we ignore at our peril. Living in the present and casting aside the negative future was starting to develop in my mind, not only responding to events in my life but in the way I wanted to *live* my life.

"... ALL THE KOOKY IDEAS WILL BE COMING AT ME ..."

While helping Lenore negotiate her treatment for breast cancer, I'm coping with my own diagnosis of prostate cancer.

I'm not qualified to know anything about cancer or its treatment, and certainly nothing about prostate cancer. In my circle, it's widely thought that I have the mind of a researcher. Some friends love to travel with me because they know I'll do all the digging on where to go and why.

Like Henry Higgins, I don't understand people who don't think like I think. Why would you go to Paris without knowing what's there before you're there? Why go into the dark night of cancer without knowing something on your own so that you're not at the mercy of information given to you by a doctor?

As I said earlier, if a doctor isn't my partner, I'm out of here. I am in charge of my own body and my own life and I want him to aid me; I don't want to mindlessly follow someone else's path.

So after trumpeting these high-blown views to myself, I think: now what the hell do I do? I don't have to think all by myself for very long. Advice starts to come out of the woodwork from friends and relatives who know someone who knows someone who had cancer and even sometimes, cancer of the prostate. Norman, Lenore's brother, calls to say that he has a friend in Palm Springs who has had prostate cancer the year before.

"He didn't have the regular surgery. I don't know what it's called but he had small seeds put in his prostate. Radioactive seeds."

"Sounds interesting," I say. I am thinking, now it starts, all the kooky ideas will be coming at me and this is just the first of them. Why wouldn't he just have the regular surgery like everyone else? And if you don't remove the prostate, it could come back to haunt you. Still, he gives me his friend's name and when I call him I get my first education on the subject.

The treatment he had is called Brachytherapy, the placing of tiny radioactive seeds directly into the prostate from the outside by means of a needle. About 60 of them. The idea that this is as good as surgery is certainly appealing, but seems ludicrous. As they say, if it seems too good to be true, odds are it is.

It turns out, I am wrong. The procedure has been around for many years. The seeds have a short half-life and quickly dissipate most of their radioactivity, but not before they have effectively destroyed the prostate and with it, presumably, the cancer cells.

But Brachytherapy has become my gold standard. It has a slightly better five-year success rate than the rest and generally less side effects.

Once more, being the one who makes the decision instead of saying the doctor knows best, has taken away much of the feeling of helplessness. I feel that I am in charge of my own destiny. I have satisfied myself that I have investigated all known treatments and have chosen the one that I feel is best for me and the one that makes me feel the most comfortable after I have made the decision. This is no time for self-doubt. Luckily, once I come to an informed conclusion, I don't tend to look back.

APPOINTMENT IN SEATTLE

Once more I have to make a decision. Where will I have it done? Instead of contacting the hospital in Texas or the one in Florida where I hear that Brachytherapy is being done regularly, I decide that in the end I am going to go with the one with the longest and best track record anyway. Since I have determined in my own mind that it is in Seattle, I contact them and make an appointment. There are two doctors there, Ragde and Grimm. Dr. Haakon Ragde is an internationally famous urologist who counted Deng Xiao Ping, the former Premier of China, among his patients.

They make the ultrasound picture exactly as I expect and show me how they intend to do the procedure. They plan to consult with each other at a later time and plot out the number of seeds and their proposed location. They estimate there will be 80 seeds which will be made out of titanium and filled with a radioactive substance called I-125. They will stay where they are implanted, presumably for life, although in a fairly short time their radioactivity will be negligible

I stay in Seattle for the rest of the day, spending my time at the waterfront which I have always enjoyed in that great city, and then fly back to Chicago the next day.

This research is another example of being one's own advocate. There was no central data source for the 'right' course of treatment. It was up to me to accept whatever information was thrown at me or to dig in and investigate what was best, at least for me.

". . . REALITY IS ONLY OUR PERCEPTION OF REALITY"

What a disgusting situation. My own cancer doesn't stress me too much. I have researched it completely and am satisfied that I am on the right course. But Lenore's is another matter. First her two surgeries, eight days apart, and then having to do both chemo and radiation. I feel bad for her, but certainly am not going to tell her.

The radiation starts near the end of March in 1993. She is afraid of it. So am I. But she keeps looking to me for reassurance and support, so I can't be anything except confident. It is a shitty game. I'm saying things I don't believe and Lenore's pretending that she believes me when I doubt she really does. But because she wants to, maybe she does.

Lenore starts on radiation 5 days a week for 6 weeks. No pain; just cumulative tiredness.

Strangely, we both get to the point that we enjoy going to radiation. It is our time that we treasure; time for the two of us to be alone and to do something together. And the fact that it is something designed to make Lenore well makes it all the more enjoyable.

A few weeks into Lenore's radiation treatment for breast cancer, I ask Adam if he wants to go along and am surprised when he agrees. Then, two weeks later, he asks if he can take Lenore alone. I am glad to comply. While she is being treated he gets into his usual mode of questioning the technicians, the physicist, and the doctor on all the facets of radiation therapy. It is his style to bore into a subject with great intensity and learn all he can about it; like father, like son. But unlike me, it is also his style to drop it as soon as he has sucked it dry of information.

Surprisingly, he doesn't do this with radiation therapy. Instead, a few weeks later, he says he'd like to go to National Lewis University in Evanston in order to become a radiation therapist. He had previously gone to the University of New Mexico for a few years. Neither Lenore nor I have a clear idea what he studied there or how many credit hours he has received. Adam is not overly forthcoming with information on such things. He reacts as if we are trying to delve into his private business whenever we ask how he is doing in school. Somehow he is able to talk N.L.U. into accepting him and transfers his credits to pursue his new passion

In the midst of the radiation treatments Lenore wants to meet the doctor who will be doing her series of chemo. Although the disease certainly frightens her, she has a lifelong pattern of attacking any problem head-on. Now, wanting to see the oncology doctor falls right into this mold.

Dr. Patel talks about the three chemo drugs he intends to use. The names are very difficult but I deliberately avoid writing them down so as not to appear being overly clinical. (On the next visit I write them down to make sure I remember them). I feel it necessary to assure Lenore that I am more interested in her than in some new subject.

It is decided that the chemo will start before the radiation ends and there will be a temporary overlap. A few weeks later

Lenore goes back in the hospital yet again, this time to have a Portacath implanted in her chest to make the chemo treatments easier on her. The chemo is inserted through the Portacath and then flows into one of the main blood lines above her heart. It will prevent some of her veins from collapsing.

This protocol, the course of treatment, continues for seven months. It is originally planned for six, but Dr. Patel prefers to err on the side of caution and adds a month. We do our best to make the most of them, trying to maintain a path which lets us appreciate life as we hadn't previously. Each day becomes more precious to us, and we consciously savor it, taking the time to be present in the moment.

On the 5th of May the radiation ends and all that remains are six more months of chemo. This is a very positive time. It seems we are beating the disease and having *only* the chemo to deal with is a relief. Much as we enjoy going to radiation together, the doubling up is more than she can put up with for very long.

When I got through writing this section, I picked up Lenore's journal notes (See Appendix A) and felt it was like two people telling a third person about a movie they saw together. The movie remains the same, and generally the synopsis is the same, but there are differences in details and outlook. Most of them come from the lens through which we view life. The important thing to realize is that our own lens is neither the only lens, nor, in many cases, an accurate lens.

What we think of as reality is only our *perception* of reality.

SURGERY IN SEATTLE FOR JACK

I'm not at all nervous about going to Seattle for the surgery in spite of the fact that I haven't been in a hospital since I was a child. The only glitch we have is that Lenore is scheduled to have a chemo treatment the week of my surgery. I don't know what to do. I certainly want Lenore to come with me to

Seattle, but on the other hand, it isn't worth it for her to miss her chemo treatment. Since I will be gone less than a week, in my own mind it seems possible that she can postpone her chemo for another week, but I feel sure that Dr. Patel will never agree with this. So I prepare a scenario in my mind—for that matter I prepare a number of scenarios—and finally decide on one with which to win my argument.

When we see Dr. Patel, I have my speech prepared to convince him that Lenore's treatment should be postponed; he ruins things when he readily agrees. He can't think of anything that will have a negative impact on her by waiting a week. I am really glad. I don't want her to go to chemo without me, and I don't want my surgery without her beside me, so this solves everything. Sometimes I build things up in my mind excessively, and if I just sit back and let them happen, life would be simpler.

I feel happy Lenore could go with me, glad to keep a balance in the relationship. She is happy that she now is supporting me. A role reversal we both appreciate. You have to be careful about getting into a victim mode or letting other people get into a victim mode. This was an excellent way to avoid it.

Instead of a general anesthetic, I receive an epidural. I drift off to sleep and eventually I slide back into consciousness, open my eyes and see one of the surgeons standing there.

I say, "Well Peter, are you ready to start?"

"No, Jack," he replies, "we're all finished. We're taking you off now to recovery."

What a pleasant surprise this is. I have none of the uncomfortable feeling after surgery that I had heard of relating to general anesthetic. Part of this is also due to having received a drug called *Verced*, which acts as an amnesiac, so that if I really did have an unpleasant time of it, I don't remember. After a little while in recovery, Lenore comes in and asks me how I am feeling and I say fine but that I am hungry. She asks the nurse what I can eat and is told anything goes. The nurse asks me what I would like and I tell her a turkey sandwich and a glass of water. A short while later these appear and I sit up in bed devouring them.

I am in Seattle for 5 days, returning feeling whacked out but confident I am on the right track with the surgery. (This has proved to be true.)

Whereas my treatment was over in April, 1993 and was a one-shot deal, Lenore's chemo continues for another 7 months after my surgery, which takes her to November 1993. Her hair falls out, and she looks dashing in hats and scarves. I am mentally exhausted but delighted that things are finally under control. My cancer is beaten and Lenore's is apparently also. We can resume living our lives.

My anchor in all this is Nicole, though she might not be aware of it. When I feel that I am surrounded with a series of negative events and am groping for something positive; she always provides this. Things are finally showing signs of stability. I feel that I can enjoy the one child I am closest to. I love them all, of course, but Adam is hard to read and to understand; sometimes I wonder if he reads and understands me. Stephanie is much easier to both read and understand, but because of her limitations it is simply not the same as dealing with an adult. Of the three, Nicole is the only level-headed grownup with whom, thank God, I can connect in a meaningful way. I treasure my connection with her and am grateful for what she is providing me in my dark hours.

By this time Nicole is planning to start at Loyola U. in the fall to begin studies for her Master's in Pediatrics. I am unbelievably proud of her. At the same time I am terribly afraid that all this background noise will affect her studies. As best I can tell, it doesn't.

Adam is starting at National Louis University, taking courses to become a radiation technician. We have our fingers crossed that this will work out for him.

How does one survive all this battering? Not easily, of course, but one survives because there is no other choice, other than jumping off the bridge. But for those of us who prefer dry land, we will manage to push on through the pain and hopefully come out somewhat whole on the other side.

Once more, where is this emotional and mental pain coming from? Mostly from fear of the unknown. Fear of the future and what might happen.

I keep coming back to the subject of *choice*. Why, after all, should we choose to live in the past and fear the future, when we can live in the present and enjoy our lives?

It would have been quite easy to focus on the terrible things that happened to Lenore in the recent past, and even easier to think about the worse things to come that were perhaps right around the corner. Instead, we were fortunate to be able to appreciate that which we had and to enjoy each other for such things as the time we spent going to radiation together.

Each of the doctors to date has treated us as joint partners with them in his or her discipline, instead of treating Lenore like a patient. The beneficial effect on her is enormous though not measurable. Surely but slowly it is becoming integrated into her way of looking at life and at her disease.

✦
LIFE RESUMES

CANCER SUPPORT GROUP

In 1994, Lenore and I join a cancer support group. It is made up of 12 people who have completed treatment for cancer. There are a number of groups in the support center; each group is limited to 12. Lenore and I are the only couple that was allowed to join together . . . . usually, spouses are not allowed . . . . because we are both cancer survivors. The organization initially was against it, but the more they thought about it, the less they could figure out a way to say no.

Support works both ways. You support the others in the group and they support you.

Eventually, you will cease to be guarded and tell anybody there about how you are feeling and thinking.

It was difficult to belong to the group because about half of the members would die. We realized this but decided it was better not to erect an emotional barrier among us. This intensified our grief when we lost a member but 'better to have loved and lost . . . . .'

The group found a way to deal with this by having a party to celebrate the deceased person's life, instead of mourning their death. Then the spot would be filled by someone on the waiting list so that there were always 12 members.

ADAM AND JACK IN SEATTLE

In January of 1994, I need to go back to Seattle for a post-op Brachytherapy checkup with Dr. Ragde. Adam asks if he can go along. I agree, but why, I don't know. I always feel that I should give it one more try, but the fact is whenever Adam goes on any kind of a trip with me, or Lenore and me, it usually ends with regrets. Adam by now has tired of his new adventure with the Mormon Church and has returned to his usage of drugs and alcohol. Friends from church did try valiantly to get him to return, to no avail. When it became apparent that they were not going to get him to change his ways, they gave up and dropped him. At this point he is a non-worker, a heavy drinker, and a drug user. Which drugs he uses are unknown to us but nothing would have surprised me. He is still enrolled in NLU, taking classes to become a radiation therapist and seems to be doing well in his studies. This is probably why I agreed for him to go with me on this trip.

When we are finished in Seattle we rent a car and drive to Vancouver. Knowing Adam's drinking habits, I carefully plan my strategy. When we get to the hotel I go to the bartender and tell him that Adam is not to charge anything to the room. I take the same precaution with room service and the restaurant. Since he has no money I congratulate myself on being clever. After being in the room for a while, he feels a need to get out and see what is going on in the lobby. I smile to myself, imagining his real reason. Forty-five minutes later Adam still hasn't returned, but it causes me no concern since he easily strikes up conversations with strangers. I turn on the TV and see that the hotel has various services available on the screen, including the ability to see an ongoing total of your bill. I try this out and am amazed to see that I already have about $40 in charges to my account. I assume that Adam has gone to the gift shop and bought something, which irritates me since he hasn't asked permission. At that point, I go down to the lobby to look for him but he is nowhere to be found. Eventually I go to the center of the atrium where there is an indoor swimming pool surrounded by a fence. Adam is sitting in a chair watching the people in the pool and holding a drink in his hand. It is a double scotch; I later find out it is his third. What I have overlooked is the fact that they have waiters at poolside to bring guests food or drink. By this time, Adam is only slightly drunk, his tolerance for alcohol being much higher than three doubles. I am furious. Together we return to the room.

TRANQUILITY

Then begin three years of relative serenity, with subjects medical mostly behind us. Things have settled down to a normal rhythm and the mundane events of everyday life come with relief. We welcome the routine that others consider boring. 'Nothing' happening is a blessing that we had felt was beyond our reach just months ago.

In the fall of 1994 Nicole meets a wonderful young man, Larry, and is now working on her Master's degree in pediatrics. I feel happy her life is coming together so nicely after all the stress of last year.

Lenore goes back to work. She resumes some independence, though she's not as aggressively independent as she had been just before her breast cancer. Still, the importance of returning to the real world is huge, in her eyes and mine. It is an important signal that the pain and the problems are behind us.

In August of 1995, Lenore arranges a 30th birthday party for Stephanie at a local hotel. There are more than 100 people there including a number of residents from the facility where she lives, Riverside Foundation, a marvelous place. Some of them have Down Syndrome, as she does, but others have various kinds of retardation, developmental disorders. There is a disk jockey, lots of food, and more presents than she could possibly ever use. Nevertheless, as so often happens, I initially think it is a foolish expense on Lenore's part at the time, but later come to regard it as one of her better ideas. The video tape from that party is one of my priceless possessions today.

We are getting used to the idea that 1995 is mercifully uneventful on the medical front.

In the Spring of 1996, Lenore wants to have her Portacath taken out. She feels the cancer is gone and since it is almost three years, I have to agree. There are no signs to the contrary, and I also think it will help her physically and mentally to have such a signal that this thing is beaten. I reason that her mind will help her keep the cancer from recurring with her positive attitude. It is a perfect example of living in the *NOW*. She was able to let go of the past cancer and its unpleasant memories. Instead, she stayed present.

In the Fall I go to Kenya on my first photo safari, an incredible experience. I would enjoy it more if Lenore would come along but that is expecting too much. She always is more a Ritz Carlton sort of person, definitely not a tent person. Even if I had succeeded in talking her into going she would be miserable. She is apprehensive about bugs and heat. Neither is a problem, but if you think things will be bad, they will be bad. But I am still comforted by the fact that I am not consumed by the bad things in life and am also able, with Lenore, to live in the present.

We have the sense of having been through tough times and made it. We no longer have to think about them and simply choose not to.

Adam, having succeeded in getting admitted to National Louis University, has done very well in his studies. But he cannot stand success. He is dropped from the program at NLU. He brings this on himself by not showing up for class, not turning in assignments, and not heeding their warnings that he couldn't continue on this way. These actions were typical of his history. He felt that he alone knew what was best and either that rules were made for others, or that rules were made to be broken. At various times he demonstrated his belief in both versions. In addition to his problems with drugs and alcohol, Adam has a problem with authority. He can't accept that others may have this authority and fights against it even when that fight is self-destructive.

Failing to complete this program confirms to Adam that he seemingly can do nothing right, nor complete anything, which once more eats away at his self-esteem, already in a low state. Lenore and I don't know how to help him cope more effectively.

Near the end of the year Nicole gets engaged to Larry. Lenore and I are very happy about it, especially since we like him very much. Lenore and Stephanie get really excited about the idea of helping Nicole to plan her wedding and start to make plans as to how they will each participate.

". . . THIS NEW BLACK FLAG ON OUR HORIZON . . ."

Everything is going along swimmingly until March of 1997. On the 19th, Lenore gets a terrific pain in the right side of her rib cage and can't imagine what it could be from. I, who love to diagnose such things, can't figure it out either. The problem is that there doesn't seem to be anything in that area other than her lung. She takes a pain pill and hopes it will go away the next day. It doesn't.

On the second day the pain seems to increase as the day wears on. It describes it as sharp, as if someone was sticking a dagger in her side. I am more concerned that yesterday but not overly since I don't know what's going on.

I say, "Maybe we'd better go have it checked out."

Lenore resists. "Oh, you always want to go to the doctor and get things checked out; it's not a problem."

I don't like doing nothing, but I figure that it's probably nothing serious. Nothing that can't be treated.

It isn't just the pain. She is having a tough time breathing. It is hard for her to take a deep breath.

At the end of the third day, the pain killers aren't doing anything and she gets out of breath walking across the room.

That night, Lenore can't stand the pain any more. She says, "All right. Let's do it your way and get it checked out."

I drive her to the ER at Lake Forest Hospital. I'm glad to get her there and have professionals making the decisions.

The doctor in charge that night comes in and listens and thumps asks her to take deep breaths which of course she can't do. He thinks it might be a blood clot. He tells us that he is sending her to x-ray to see what is going on.

The doctor returns and tells us that he has just looked at the films of her chest and they confirm his suspicions. It isn't lung cancer; it is a blood clot. I ask what will be done to correct this and the doctor says he is putting her on a blood thinner called *Coumadin*. It is only a matter of time before the clot is dissolved and the pain will be gone. We are both greatly relieved that it is no big deal. Lenore and I are satisfied. "Yeah. OK. Thank God you discovered it and everything is fine."

But then he says, this isn't addressing the problem. Where did the clot come from and why? He schedules her for a CT scan the next day.

The next morning we go back to Lake Forest for the test and that afternoon Dr. Patel calls. "That was Dr. Patel," I say, "and he says he has bad news and good news."

"Give me the bad news first."

"I'll give you both at once. The blood clot was caused by a tumor on one of your ovaries. The good news is that it can't be very old since it wasn't there in November, according to Dr. Shewitz, I think he feels that the problem is correctable." I think: It's either recent and fast growing or he missed it in November. (The latter would be good news.)

"How is it correctable?"

"Surgery. He made an appointment for us to see Dr. Beck tomorrow," I reply. "He's a surgeon and Dr. Patel seems to think he knows what he's doing."

"Is this terrible news?" she asks, probably trying not to let her voice show how scared she is.

"Doesn't look like it," I answer. "Since it's new I'm guessing it's small and it will just be one more hurdle to get over." I am desperately trying to appear clinical and unconcerned and think I probably succeed. The fact is this is nothing to be unconcerned about. It just seems the right thing to say in spite of how I feel. I feel the fear of the unknown again. I don't know if the cancer has spread.

I think, "Holy shit! Here we go again!"

I'm scared again. Not unduly concerned, but enough.

We meet the doctor. "Is this a very new tumor?" I ask.

"Hard to say," the doctor replies. "Dr. Shewitz saw nothing there late last year when you were in and now the damned thing is there. I have to assume it's new."

"Can we also assume that it's small and controllable?"

At that point I detect the smallest hesitation on his part. But then I think he made his decision that we wanted to hear everything.

"I don't have any idea if it's controllable, but it's not that small. The tumor is 8cm."

"How big is that in inches?" I ask.

"It looks like it's a little more than three inches in diameter," he replies.

I am startled. Three inches in diameter would make it about the size of Lenore's fist! I am also getting the feeling that he is regarding this whole thing as a grave situation. He doesn't say so in so many words, but the look on his face doesn't seem too optimistic.

I ask, "What's the prognosis?"

"Depends on what we find. We need to do a complete hysterectomy. I'd like to do it as soon as possible. I think this thing is a fast grower and there's nothing to be gained by waiting."

"When can you do it?"

"I could do it in the morning. Dr. Shewitz could assist me. Is that all right with you?"

I think, 'Here we go again'. I am more scared than the first time.

On Lenore's breast cancer, the doctors were saying this is a young tumor and the chances are really good.

On the ovarian cancer, they are implying this is a young tumor and things are really bad because it is so new and so big.

After the surgery, Dr. Beck stops in to see how Lenore is doing and tells us where we go from here. He says the diagnosis is Stage III-C Ovarian Cancer and that Dr. Patel will discuss the chemo that we will need to beat this thing. They reinsert a Portacath during the surgery for just this purpose.

What worries me is that the surgeon never says we've caught it and things ought to be all right. He doesn't look like things are going to be all right either: he always looks dead serious.

While there is a fear of the unknown here, there is also the look on his face – a fear of the known.

I start to deal with this fear of the unknown. I hope I'll be able to say, "We've got a really bad thing going on here. But what's going to happen in the future is that it is beatable."

I become the investigator. I need to find out the stats on ovarian cancer. In cancer, everything depends on how early you catch it in relation to its rate of growth. We just don't know where we are with Lenore's.

Lenore and I have a discussion as to what to tell the kids. We decide to tell Stephanie nothing for the foreseeable future. We feel that Adam and Nicole are tougher and can deal with it. But the more we think about this, the sillier it seems. Few people are that tough. How they seem and how they really are, are two different matters.

The proof of this is Adam's reaction. We sit down with him and tell him all we know. He acts as if we are telling him about going to someone's birthday party. Mild interest, but little emotional involvement. As the years go by I think back to that conversation and realize it was simply part of his shell, his armor. Nicole, of course, is another matter. She is just as attached to Lenore and never minds letting her distress show. But even in her case I feel that she is showing less than she feels, to protect Lenore.

Both are equally probing in their questions, wanting to know about the treatment, prognosis, doctors and so forth. I think getting 100% of the facts, *as we know them,* is a form of comfort to them.

There is a tension between the need I feel to put on a very positive face for Lenore and my own doubts, concerns, and fears. I feel she is relying on me to be the strong one who is going to see that we win this battle, so I don't want to admit doubts. Stephanie isn't intellectually capable of talking about these issues and Adam isn't emotionally capable of it. I don't want to burden Nicole.

I am left feeling very isolated and lonely at times.

Just when you think everything is under control, life happens. More than three years after the end of the breast cancer treatment, and we were lulled into ongoing optimism. You simply don't think that a pain in the side of your rib cage is going to be anything serious. And when you're called back to reality, it is with a jolt.

Sometimes it seems like the cumulative battering from one thing after another is worse than any single event.

After Lenore had successfully beaten her breast cancer and after I had eliminated my prostate cancer, we were imagining that it was very difficult, but that it was now all behind us and that we were lucky that we dealt with it and could now get on with our lives.

However, having this new black flag on our horizon was extremely disconcerting. It felt like we just couldn't win. I felt sorry for Lenore and I felt sorry for me. The fact that I determined that I shouldn't tell her either of these made me feel isolated. A person needs to talk to someone in times of stress. Lenore had me. I had no one, because I chose it that way.

Much of the mental strain here was in trying to maintain a façade of strength when I really felt like a tower of weakness. It would have been easier if I had learned in my childhood that it was all right to exhibit fear in some situations. But to feel that, at all times, I have to be stronger than anyone else, is a terrible burden, since I knew that it wasn't true.

There are times when women have an advantage over men since they are frequently more able to express their emotions. In later years this charade can break down when the man in a relationship incurs deep stress and, being unused to expressing his feelings, grows more dependent on his spouse to teach him how to do so.

"WE FEEL THAT THE THING HAS FINALLY BEEN BEATEN"

The nightmare restarts. It seems like some sort of cosmic cancer plot. Lenore has beaten her breast cancer; I have beaten mine. Now we are back in the soup. The ovarian cancer is a whole new ball game. Supposedly it is not connected with the breast cancer, but I think that it couldn't be a coincidence. There is no way one person can contract a whole new cancer without it being some way related to the first. In my mind it is either genetic or it is caused by smoking. I can't tell Lenore about my smoking theory because she already feels I am paranoid about the subject and tend to blame half the medical problems in the world on it. I still feel this way. Smoking and other things are related to your environment and are the root cause of more than half of the so-called diseases we call 'natural', as in: He died of natural causes. Maybe the person hasn't been shot, but the death isn't natural either. If one insults the body, the body will react and get even.

Another surgery. Another! Thoughts go through my head frequently such as: 'When will it end?' Better yet, 'How will it end?' I make it more difficult because I believe that I can't discuss these thoughts with Lenore. At times, my self-induced silence crushes me. She voices similar concerns, but I feel obliged to steer her in the opposite direction. It's easy enough to have concerns bordering on panic if you're the person with the disease. But my job, as I see it, is to support; sometimes to tell the truth about what I am thinking and at other times to express an optimism that I just don't have.

People think that there is a monolithic disease called Cancer. It is actually about 300 separate diseases. Ovarian cancer is totally different than Breast cancer, for example, and just because they are both cancers, there is no other connection. In turn, the chemos used to fight them are many and varied. Each is tailored for the specific type of cancer. The bad things which go along with each combination change even from person to person, depending on how you tolerate them. The fact is that if these drugs are used long enough, they will destroy your immune system. But this is a subject about which you will hear little.

Throughout all this, it could be easy to lose sight of Nicole's feelings. Her mother's second cancer; Adam's problems; Stephanie's ongoing health concerns. By this time my head is swimming and I have to make sure that she isn't lost in the shuffle of my mind.

As the months go by, Nicole is a calming influence on me; it helps enormously that she is able to maintain her equilibrium in the face of these disasters.

It might very well be that she is as shook up as I, but I prefer to take it at face value and assume that she is able to keep her head when perhaps others can't. This relationship with Nicole is of tremendous importance to me. Simply the ability to not lose the connection with healthy members of the family when focusing on illness is a treasure beyond words. We are able to maintain a mutual support, along with the relationship that is not only illness-centered.

Chemo starts. A small amount of hair falls out about three weeks into the treatment. Then more. Eventually it is falling out in clumps and Lenore is reluctant to even look at her pillow in the morning for fear of what she'll find. Soon enough she reaches the point of asking me to shave it all off and get it over with. We go out on to the patio and I use clippers to do the job effectively and neatly, except for some clean-up work with a razor. Her attitude about this latest blow to her pride is far better than mine would be if I were in her shoes. My hair is thin; hers is gorgeous. But she bears this with stoical dignity. She goes to a wig store and buys three wigs which she delights in. One is long and blondish and I think she looks awful in it, but she likes the look so much that I never tell her so. The other two are shorter and in different colors. I don't think she has much intention of wearing them regularly, but I do think they are a security blanket for her, knowing that she doesn't have to go out bald. She also wears scarves which are specifically designed for women in chemo. But barring that, she seems most comfortable wearing a baseball cap. The important thing is that there are avenues open to her; the wigs, the scarves, and the baseball caps are there to ward off the stares from people on the street. Eventually she doesn't mind these either. At other times she simply goes out with her head bare.

While Lenore is undergoing chemotherapy for ovarian cancer, she also helps plan and shop for Nicole's wedding. This keeps her engaged in life. Lenore and Nicole feel very close as they make these preparations. Stephanie gets involved, too. She goes on the shopping trips. She loves it. The three of them try on beautiful dresses, pick the best ones, and get them fitted.

Nicole and Larry get married in September, 1997 in a marvelous ceremony in an art gallery in Chicago. Stephanie is the maid of honor. She is ecstatic with all the preparation and the ceremony itself. The rest of us are able to put our problems behind us and to concentrate on simply being present in the moment.. Lenore is beautiful and radiant despite the effects of her chemo which have made her face puffy and her head bald. She gets dressed up and wears a big hat. She is feeling better physically at this time, and she's delighted with the wedding. She is able to feel this time of joy in the midst of difficulties. Nicole is a lovely bride.

Lenore's chemo starts out with the second treatment right behind the first by two weeks. Then they are spaced every three weeks apart. I notice signs from the doctors and from the nurses in the oncology office and when I put them together I decide that we are dealing with a different sort of beast here than breast cancer. This is scarier. I felt signals with the breast cancer, signals that the cancer was new and could probably be brought under control, regardless of the unpleasantness in between. But this is something else. I hear no signals of confidence, only wariness. This is something much harder to tame. I know we are in for a long, hard fight. I don't like the feel of it.

I can feel that we are now standing in the ever-lengthening shadows of mortality.

I wonder now about the underlying philosophy when first confronting a disease. It's very possible that some, or all, of Lenore's doctors knew from the very first day that it is a lost cause.

Dr. Patel's only weakness, as nearly as I can tell, is the inability to answer a question straight out. He avoids the tough ones. When Lenore asks him what her chances are of survival, he replies that only God knows the answer, but that he will do everything in his power to make sure that she receives the best care. Depending on your outlook, this might seem a perfectly reasonable reply. It is not my outlook; if anything, it results in lessening one's hope of survival. I cannot *imagine* Bernie Siegel responding in this way. What I *can* imagine as his answer is this: "In the face of uncertainty, there is nothing wrong with hope." As he says in *Love, Medicine & Miracles*, "To create a relationship of trust, the doctor and patient must learn each other's beliefs. When a doctor can instill some measure of hope, the healing process sometimes starts even before treatment begins."

Lenore gets a blood test, CA 125, specific to ovarian cancer, every month to check on the progress of the disease. The normal count for a woman, even without cancer, is less than 32. Hers rises to 201 in the earlier part of 1997. But by the end of December the count has dropped to 31. The chemo has finally kicked in.

"What a Hanukkah present!" she says. "I have to tell you, I was plenty worried. And that chemo is a real pain. I never really believed it would work. But now look!"

"Why would you think it wouldn't work?" I ask. "It worked four years ago on the breast cancer. There's no reason to think it wouldn't work on this one." I don't believe a word I am saying, but she does.

"It's a completely different drug, a different combination. Anyway, it's a different cancer. How did we know it would work?"

Obviously, the chemo is working. The fact that the number has fallen to one point less than normal is quite a relief. We feel that the thing has finally been beaten. All the surgery and months of chemo, as unpleasant as they were, have paid off and that is more important.

✚

THE REALLY
BAD NEWS

ADAM: ALCOHOL, DRUGS
AND SELF-DESTRUCTION

As I mentioned earlier, as Adam's years from 17 to 27 went by he had many perceived problems and, in his mind, resolved most of them with either drugs or alcohol. Sometimes both.

One day after drinking he physically attacks his girlfriend Cori and she calls the police. He is arrested and confined to Cook County Jail, where he spends the next two months. We had a life-long habit of bailing him out of his problems. This time we are determined to have him experience the consequences of his actions.

Easy to say, but grinding experience to do. Thinking of him in that filthy jail with filthy people. When I went to visit him there it was very bad, feeling that I was partly to blame for him being there, responsible for him staying there, since we had a choice that he could leave if we put up bail.

We are able to get him released after this period on condition that he gets formal treatment for his problems.

Because we were never happy that he was in jail, we are greatly relieved that he is getting out. It was a good idea that he went to jail but we didn't like it. Not with the inmates I saw there when I visited.

He enters a program called Interventions which is designed for people who drink too much. I feel relief that he might be getting some help from them, but I am dubious.

He is required to stay there until they determine he is fit to leave. . It is not a locked facility; he can leave, but the people in charge threaten to call the police if he walks out the door.

His stay there lasts only a month at which time he decides he has had enough. Not feeling constrained by the norms of authority figures, he walks out anyway, fully expecting to be picked up shortly. Instead he manages to get to an expressway and hitchhikes to our house.

Since he doesn't have a key and no one is home, he breaks a basement window and is waiting for me in the kitchen when I return. I am, of course, startled but try to look otherwise because I feel that startled is the look he is expecting, if not hoping for. Nevertheless, in spite of how I look on the outside, I am quite nervous about this turn of events, knowing that Adam is either going to be rearrested, or might do something totally crazy to prevent that from happening.

I am on one side of the kitchen and Adam is sitting on the other next to the phone. I notice that a number of bottles of Lenore's prescription drugs are out of the cabinet and on the counter. I ask him if he knows why they are out there. He replies that he is feeling suicidal and that he has taken a large number of various drugs including a lot of Klonopin. I immediately stride across the kitchen, pick up the phone and dial 911. Adam asks what I am doing and I tell him I am calling an ambulance. He tells me to put down the phone. When I look he is pointing a pistol at my face. I have no doubt the gun is loaded because it is mine, and I am afraid that he will certainly shoot me. I had the pistol in my bedroom in a locked steel box which was bolted to the floor. He somehow broke it open before I came home.*

---

* Ten years later I had an epiphany. It had never occurred to me before but one day I realized why he went to such trouble to get my pistol out of such a secure place. It was to kill himself! This came to me while reading an article on suicide in the NY Times. It said that guns were not frequently used by people planning suicide; but had one of the highest rates of 'success' of those who actually killed themselves. They pointed out that if a person was interrupted in his mission, for instance if the bullets were in a second location and he had to spend time looking for them, the suicide attempt was frequently put off for another day. I think Adam spent so much time and trouble tearing the box apart he became frustrated and put off suicide for another day. At least with a gun.

Having spent two years in the Korean War, I have an intimate knowledge, fear, and respect of firearms. I am terrified, feeling that my life might end at any moment. I put down the phone. A short while later 911 calls back and asks if there is a problem. Adam says it was dialed in error and they accept this answer. I am relieved and horrified at the same time, thinking that nothing I can imagine is going to relieve this impasse.

Just then, Lenore comes home with various nieces. Adam tucks the pistol under his shirt in his rear waistband and nonchalantly leaves with them for a trip to a large shopping mall. I am too afraid to tell Lenore that Adam has the gun for fear he will pull it out and create a situation that will be potentially fatal. On the other hand, I am feeling like a coward, to not bring the matter to a head.

As I watch them leave, I fear for him, I fear for Lenore and the girls, and I fear for strangers at the mall who don't have no idea that there is somebody out there not clicking on all cylinders who had a loaded pistol. Who knows what could trigger him to use the gun? I imagine scenarios in which a security guard approaches them, perhaps to tell them of some construction further into the mall. Adam sees a uniform and panics. He pulls out the pistol. The guard pulls out his. One of them fires and any one of a number of people could get hit. This fear was very real. I was terrified that there could be a tragedy

After they leave, I call police in Buffalo Grove. They ask me to come to the police station. We determine a course of action. They need to find a way to hold onto Adam and at same time, get the gun away from him. Because it was illegal for Adam to leave Interventions, it smoothes the way for them to be involved. We are agreed that I should go to the mall with the police, find the car, and look in it to see if the gun is there. After much searching in the huge parking lot, we find the car; the pistol is in the trunk.

I am tremendously relieved that the gun is now in police hands. But a new worry takes over: how will Adam be arrested? Will there be a horrible struggle? I don't want Adam to be hurt. I also realize that Lenore will be greatly pissed since she doesn't know about the gun.

As the group exits one of the stores, I am sitting in an unmarked car with policeman to point out Adam. I was doing what I needed to do but didn't like it. Although I was a main participant, I had no idea what was going to happen, nor could I control it. Just waiting for something to happen was nerve wracking.

I point him out and the police arrest him. He puts up no resistance. One policeman told Adam, we have to arrest you. Adam told policeman OK, I'm ready. He was handcuffed and led off by the police.

I am relieved that the outcome was resolved peacefully, without the mayhem that could have happened. Lenore is furious that I have done this without including her in the decision. The illogic of this doesn't occur to her. I was hoping for, 'Wow, this must have been really tough for you, turning in our son. Thanks.' Instead, I got, 'You SOB.' That hurt even though I knew it was coming.

My lack of logic doesn't occur to me; Lenore had no idea about the gun when Adam was arrested. Why wouldn't she be upset?

I am sorry Lenore feels the way she does, but I am results-driven and I can accept her anger in order to obtain the safe conclusion that came about, out of danger's way. Only when it is over do I realize that the tightness in my chest and stomach have dissolved. The realization comes only in the *absence* of the tension.

I am hurt that Lenore remains angry even after she hears about the gun at the police station. I picture myself as the 'Wounded white knight'. I'm the good guy. I come riding in on a white horse and someone knocks me off. How could *I* be the bad guy?

Someone comes to the police station and evaluates Adam. Determining that he is a danger to himself and others, he is transferred from there to a state mental hospital in Elgin, Illinois, where he is expected to work out his dysfunctions with society by means of psychotherapy. He is in Elgin for a couple of months. Lenore and I visit him once a week. At first there doesn't seem to be any improvement, but gradually he appears to be behaving normally.

At the end of this time, Adam is making plans for leaving Elgin and deciding what to do with his life. He seems more at peace and, for all intents and purposes, has stopped using drugs and alcohol. He is nice to be with. The happiness that has too long been absent I now feel. My love for him never left but it is now a pleasure to have it and our happiness unimpeded. My feelings haven't been this warm in a long time.

I pick him up from the hospital on a Saturday in January for a weekend leave. He tells me that the psychiatrist wants to know if Lenore and I will be interested in coming out to Elgin for a conference. This would include Adam, and the goal would be to determine a future course of action. When I say that I'd be very interested, Adam seems surprised, although I have no idea why. I immediately feel that the reason he is surprised shows how communication between us is near zero. It might be a sign of the detachment that exists between us, hearing what the other is saying but unable to process the meaning. If he doesn't understand that we want to go, there is a complete disconnect makes me wonder how long we've been disconnecting. This feels very bad; very sad.

SUICIDE

That evening he and his friend Mara go out and get home around midnight. An hour or two later they wake me up with loud talking and cabinet doors slamming. I am quite irritated and go downstairs to let them know that they have awakened me and ask them to be quiet. They sound quite contrite and promise to be quieter. A few hours later, Adam appears at my bedroom door and I ask him, in an aggravated way, what he wants. He mentions that Mara isn't there anymore. I ask,

"What are you doing?" He says, "I'm looking for Fergie. I am locking the dogs up overnight." I say, "Fergie is here with us sleeping. Couldn't you just lock up the other two?" He asks again and I shoo Fergie off in Adam's direction. I ask him to please go to sleep. I am pissed. He is obviously just wandering around.

His actions would have been considered abnormal for most other people, but for Adam it was virtually part of his pattern. In spite of this, I am feeling quite edgy. I feel it is just one more example of his self-absorption, not noticing the effect that his actions have on other people. Lenore sleeps thru all this.

At 7:00 in the morning I go downstairs. The first thing I notice is that the gates we use to keep the dogs in the kitchen are missing, which is peculiar. My personal radar is immediately on red alert. The dogs aren't where they are supposed to be and the gates are missing. Something is very wrong and I don't know what it is. I have only seconds to react, but in this short period of time, I experience a combination of fear and anger. Between the kitchen and the garage is the laundry room. I assume the dogs are in there.

I enter the laundry room and in a split second notice two things: the dogs aren't in there and I hear the car in the garage running. I'm afraid I know what that means. The unknown lurks on the other side of that wall and I don't want to confront it. But I have no choice. Opening the door to the garage I am met by a huge cloud of exhaust smoke. I open the overhead door and can see Adam in the driver's seat of Lenore's Lincoln to my right. He is seated upright with his head leaning back. I race around the rear of the car to his door to turn the car off. The door is partly opened and his left foot is on the ground. I reach inside the door and find that it isn't the Lincoln that's running. With that I run to my van in the adjoining space and I discover it is the engine I hear. I turn it off. I race back into the house and call 911. I am much too involved in damage control to be scared.

The operator gets the basic information from me and pro-
ceeds to ask me a series of inane questions, such as, 'How old
is he?' I tell her they'll find out when they get here.

I slam the phone down and go back into the garage to
Adam, where I give him mouth to mouth resuscitation. I ab-
sently notice that the skin on his arm and neck has small white
blotches on it. I feel that he is probably dead. I am sick to my
stomach and am afraid that I will throw up at this critical
moment, but I must not. I have to continue. I force myself to
concentrate on reviving Adam. I cannot afford to give in to the
light-headed feeling that is washing over me. At the same time
I want to escape and think that I could do so if I passed out.

A short time later, the ambulance comes roaring down the
street and the paramedics come in and take over. I realize later
that I felt a wave of relief when they came in and someone
other than I was in charge. I didn't want to be in charge of
Adam if he was dead.

They ask if there is anyone else in the house. When I tell
them Lenore is, they ask if I want them to tell her what is going on. I say no, that I will. Immediately behind them come the
firemen and the police.

When I get upstairs Lenore is sitting on the john. I sit on
the edge of the bathtub, about four feet from her. She has no
clue what is happening.

I say, "Remember a few months ago when Adam tried to
kill himself with your pills?"

When she says yes, I say, "Well this time he tried again and
I think he might have succeeded." I feel he is probably dead,
but I want to let her absorb this one step at a time instead of
telling her what I think straight out. I was afraid she would go
to pieces, but she doesn't react as one might expect, probably
because she is in shock. Instead, she simply says, 'Uh, oh!' At
that moment, I realize that I am probably in shock myself.
I was an active participant in an unreal situation. This was
not connected to the real world. The horror of what is happening is taking over for me also. She reacts calmly to what I

am telling her. We go downstairs because the paramedics and now the firemen want us out of the house. When I opened the door to the garage, I filled the house with carbon monoxide. They won't let us exit through the garage, directing us instead through the front door.

I am standing on the snow-covered driveway, trying desperately to control a situation that is way beyond control and needing to protect Lenore in a situation in which she cannot be protected. I want to cry. I want to sit down in the middle of the driveway and cry. But I force myself not to. "Boys don't cry," my father said. At this late age, I still believe him.

I look around at the cold deserted street and keep thinking 'ordinary'. Until minutes ago, this was an ordinary day, to be filled with ordinary events and ordinary conversations. It wasn't supposed to be like this. Something had gone badly wrong with the rules. You simply don't get up at 7:00 on a Sunday morning to face something so totally unexpected. Horribly and monstrously unexpected. I feel this is completely unacceptable; but 'acceptable' isn't one of my options.

By this time, they have taken Adam out of the garage and he is in the ambulance, parked at the curb. I find it hard to believe that my son is in that vehicle and that I am standing here watching it all like a spectator. I feel that I am disassociated from the events swirling around me. The paramedics are totally noncommittal and poker faced. I can see them through the small window in the ambulance, working furiously, but the size of the window prevents me from seeing what is happening otherwise. The ambulance stays right where it is without leaving. It takes a few minutes for me to realize it is standard procedure to get a patient stabilized before taking off. We call Lenore's sister Helene and her husband Bob, and they come over. Because it is freezing out, and because we can't go back in the house until the fumes are cleared out, we sit in their car for a while. Then we go to a local convenience store for coffee, trying, I suppose, to perform some mundane act that might center us. By the time we get back, the ambulance is gone. One of the firemen tells us he found the dogs locked in the basement and has released them.

We go back into the house. Police and firemen are still there, working to make sure the last vestige of fumes is gone. A policeman sits at the small round glass table in the kitchen filling out a report. I am nervous as a cat, virtually twitching with nervous energy, at times sitting on the kitchen counter, then getting off to feed the dogs, looking out the window at nothing, and generally trying to have something physical to do. I don't feel I am really there. I have no remembrance what Lenore is doing all this time. I am feeling totally useless. Nothing I can do for Adam, nothing I can do for Lenore. I feel irrelevant and hopeless.

When one of the other policemen comes back to the house an hour or so later to report that Adam has indeed died, it is an anticlimax, even though his death hadn't been confirmed until then.

At that moment I am staring at the phone, realizing that there is something that I must do: call Nicole and tell her that her brother is dead. I simply don't want to do this; I don't want to be me. But there is no choice. I go to the office on the main floor to make the call. I need to be alone. It is the next to worst thing that happens that day. And then I die inside. I am tremendously sorry for Nicole for what she is about to hear; I am vastly sorry for myself for what I have to tell her.

I ask Nicole if she remembers that Adam tried to kill himself a few months back? Well, I say, this time he might have succeeded. *Might have succeeded, she asks, or did succeed*? I am unprepared for such a question and manage to stammer out that he did succeed. She starts to reply but in the middle of a sentence, she suddenly hangs up. I'm not sure that she understood what I told her and so call back. Larry answers and says Nicole can't talk to you right now; she's hysterical. My first thought is to envy her ability to cry. At times like this I wish I couldn't function. But I do.

I am sagging with relief that this is now behind me, it was done; feeling that anyone else I had to call can't be this bad.

The next day I am determined that I must get into the Lincoln right then and there or I might never get in it again. I go into the garage and stand outside the car, trying to bring myself to open the driver's door. I can't. Instead, I burst out crying and put my arm on top of the car and my head cradled on my arm. I don't want to be there. I don't want to be in my own skin. I am overwhelmed by the unfairness of my situation. I feel that I am starting to drown in things I don't want to do. Summoning the remnants of my will power, I open the door and force myself into the driver's seat, start the engine, and drive around the block. For the next two years, I cannot bear to have a car running while warming up in a garage. I ask people to move their car outside and let it warm up out there, whether at my house or theirs.

A month later it occurs to me that we hadn't gone to the hospital with Adam. A month later. We must have been that sure of the inevitable. Where, I ask myself, have I been for the past month?

For a long time thereafter I am unable to come downstairs on Sunday mornings before 8:00, avoiding the nightmare that 7:00 Sunday morning represents for me. Instead, I lie in bed, eyes open and staring at the ceiling. Remembrance of what has happened, and fear of the unknown future, have overtaken me. For that hour each week I am effectively paralyzed. I say nothing to anyone about this. It is a small temporary prison of my own construction.

That afternoon I go to the funeral home to make the arrangements. Not sure if Lenore and Helene were along; they might have been.

I can't just ask somebody else to do this. How do I know they're going to do it right. It's too important to me. It would be easier to ask someone else, but not possible.

Adam died on Sunday and we had the funeral on Wednesday, giving people in California and other places time to come in. Adam was cremated and we had the urn with his ashes on a table at the front of the room surrounded by about 50 photos of him in various stages of his life. A minister from the Unity Church conducted the ceremony and then about 10 people got up and said nice things about Adam. The minister recited the 23rd Psalm but changed it from 'my' to 'your'. He turned to the urn containing Adam's ashes and said, "The Lord is your shepherd, you shall not want, etc." Lenore, Nicole and I wrote something also but none of us could read it and had friends do it for us. All in all, a beautiful funeral

This whole experience made Lenore and me bitter about two things: psychiatrists and the Mormon Church. Adam was living at the Elgin State Hospital in the care of supposedly accomplished psychiatrists. They felt that he not only was capable of making home visits but had scheduled him for permanent discharge, saying he was essentially cured. None of them saw the suicide coming. But that's why they're in business. It seems to me that if they couldn't recognize this in advance, what was it they're doing exactly?

I was very angry with the Mormon Church. When he died maybe three people from the church showed up.

I felt that, in destroying himself, Adam had destroyed my future. My future was to be his savior; his future was to be saved. Many others had given up on him but I never did. He had many faults and many problems, but I knew in my heart that together we would find a solution. The fact that now a solution would never more be possible was completely deflating. Like a slap in the face because he was denying me the ability to save him; depriving me of my ability and dream to bringing him back to normal, saying, in effect, 'I'm not going to let you bring me back to normal, not going to let you try again'. It was hard to reconcile that I had lost and that it was not debatable. Accepting defeat has never been one of my strengths, gracefully or otherwise.

His low self-esteem resulted in his conclusion that his life was shit. I could have – but never did – have a conversation with him, saying, 'Leave town, get a job, change your name if you need to. You could start a new life, be who you invent yourself to be, be someone other people admire'. But I didn't have that conversation. If I did, it probably wouldn't have made a difference.

I think of his death and one word trumps the rest: unacceptable. I will not accept it. But the choice isn't mine to make. Life doesn't care if I accept it or not. It just is.

I now had to come to terms with myself and the realization that I had somehow let him down. My mantra immediately after was, "What did I do wrong?" The answer, of course, was nothing. It is something akin to survivors' guilt, feeling that because something went wrong, it must be my fault. And I never thought 'we', excusing Lenore from any potential blame.

My son, my wounded bird, was beyond my saving now. I needed to put this nightmare behind me and move on with my life. But it simply hurt too much. Adam thought his life was one of failure and now I felt I was a failure for letting him down. The frustrating thing is I don't know where I failed him. I am simply fixated on the result, and the result is that he killed himself. I am virtually unable to function, holding in my hands a *fait accompli* that I always knew could happen but refused to believe *would* ever happen. I can't forgive Adam for what he has done and I can't forgive myself for not forgiving him.

Waves of pain and guilt have taken over my life. They come and they go, but when they are here, I am drowning. My grief is consuming me and I don't know what to do about it. I do know, however, that I must do something or I won't survive. I have no one to turn to. I don't want to tell Lenore or Nicole of my suffering, feeling they have enough grief of their own to want to hear anything of mine.

One small step at a time I begin to move forward, trying to live in the present instead of the past; succeeding for a few days and then falling back to my old ways on the next. But you see it wasn't yet part of me. In order to make it become so I have to practice it. I soon learn that I have to practice it every day. It doesn't come naturally. But I know that one day it will. One day it will become part of my essence.

Why did Adam kill himself? There is no answer. You are what you do. The complexity of his makeup is beyond my ability to define. Maybe a neurochemical imbalance? One ingredient, perhaps, is that he sensed a modicum of control in this act that he didn't have otherwise.

Adam felt that he had no control over his life. He lived in the past and feared the future. He had, of course, never heard of the concept of living in the joy of the present. There are things in life for which we need to recognize as controllable or not-controllable; Adam couldn't understand this difference. For years, he tried escaping life, reliving what went before and fearing what lay ahead.

When he was as young as five years old, we had taken Adam to a psychologist, to no avail. Neither the psychologist, nor we, could determine a plan that would benefit Adam.

This is what it said in his suicide note: "Dad, I don't want you to think that this is a result of anger. It was at first, but I calmed down and tried to rationalize it. The only thing I know is failure. I go to sleep every night with nightmares and wake to them every morning. My last note tells the rest. You both did a great job but something just went wrong.

I love you <u>forever</u>,

Adam

P.S. Tell Mara I fulfilled my promise. I hugged her bye, and said goodbye on the phone."

Excerpt from Lenore's journal:

He is dead. My youngest, my baby, my Adam is dead. Thank God no one said it is all for the best or I would have hit them.

He had his problems and we had them with him. The drugs, the alcohol, the lack of friends — and those he did have weren't the best. No ambition. Using us and our feelings for him to move through the world without working.

Adam's suicide was the most shattering thing in my life. They always say that the worst thing you could imagine is to lose a child. But I think people say this in the hope that it will never happen, and if they say it then maybe it won't happen. No one, including me, could ever imagine it would happen. And then it did. Actually, as bad as I feel, I feel worse for Jack. I can't imagine what he went through, finding Adam in the garage that way. I think about it and I sometimes think I know what it must have been like, but then I realize that I will never know the feeling and I don't want to know.

I sometimes wonder if one of the reasons he committed suicide was because of my cancer. He might have assumed that I was going to die and just didn't want to deal with it; he didn't want to be here when it happened. I have no way of knowing, but I hope this isn't one of his reasons. Things like this are tough enough without having to guess someone else's motives.

Suicide, for Adam, was the climax of at least ten years of suffering. It was his choice as to how to relieve that suffering. Lenore and I saw no logic in it, but it made perfect sense to him. However simplistic it sounds, he was no longer there for the debate. We couldn't ask him, nor tell him, that killing himself was a foolish and unnecessary step. But to a tortured mind, it was not foolish and was certainly necessary.

(The last person to be with Adam the night he died was his friend, Mara. In the summer of 2001, three and one-half years after Adam, Mara also killed herself.

Before this, I had asked her repeatedly to tell me about the events of that last evening. She said she would do so one day but that she was too distraught to do so now. I accepted this each time. Unfortunately, after she died the information left with her.)

I had writer's block for at least three months before starting to write this chapter. It didn't occur to me at that time, but I was obviously trying to postpone bringing up the memory. I was faced with the choice of confronting the pain of the past or simply letting my mind go blank. Unconsciously or not, the latter became my choice.

The idea of allowing ourselves to grieve was not optional. Because we were devastated, drowning in our anguish, we had no choice except to let it happen. Contrary to logic, the pain of the grief in some ways was a form of pain relief, in that it felt like there was a large reservoir of torment that needed to be drained somehow. Each episode of grieving tapped into this reservoir and allowed it to lessen, however miniscule the amount.

This form of grieving is different than any other that comes from sudden death, such as a heart attack. The amount of pain seems to be increased by the fact that suicide is a voluntary act, usually not asking for, nor respecting the thoughts of the survivors. A victim of a heart attack had no choice and would have preferred otherwise. The family and friends of a suicide victim, on the other hand, are further burdened by the fact that not only was it a choice, but that it seemed like a rejection. A rejection of the very people who must now carry on with the knowledge that they no longer have the opportunity to discuss the merits of not killing oneself.

The grief felt by these survivors must be experienced in order to have it drained. At this point, consciously accept the idea that this is the beginning of the end. Your loved one has killed himself or herself. You must not let that act also destroy *you*. You need to start the next phase of your life, though you never imagined previously that there you would ever *have* a next phase.

Those friends and relatives the suicide victim leaves behind frequently ask themselves why it happened. There is no answer to this question. The exercise is futile.

Eventually, you need to move past anger. You need to move past guilt. You will then allow yourself to come to compassion for your loved one whose view of life was so narrow that he or she could not see any alternatives to ending it. The prism they were looking through is simply different from the lens of logic we have that seems so clear.

LENORE

In February 1998, Lenore is scheduled to go to Africa with her brother and sister. After Adam's death she feels completely deflated and doesn't want to go. She is pressed by her siblings to go because it would be a great change and would temporarily take her mind off the horror of January. I join in the effort, telling her that nothing could be gained by staying home and that she could take private time on the trip to grieve. Finally she consents and they fly to Newark, where they take a chartered flight to England and then to Luxor, Egypt. For a nominal sum they are able to upgrade to Business Class which makes the flights much more pleasant. This is the same area in Egypt where a number of tourists were massacred a few months before, but the security that is added makes them feel more comfortable rather than oppressed.

From Luxor they fly to Nairobi and go on a safari for a few days. Luckily, Lenore is able to get away from the locale of Adam's death for a while to try to relax her mind. She is also able to be away from the medical part of her life and not have to worry about constant test results.

When Lenore gets back, it is as if part of the weight has been lifted from her. She has enjoyed the trip enormously, separating herself from the reality of her illness. Replacing it with the new, albeit temporary reality, she brings a degree of tranquility into her life. But even a new temporary reality is beneficial, bringing with it a recognition of living in the present, and the possibility, thereby, of a therapeutic result.

A month later, after her return from Africa in mid-March, she is retested and finds that the CA 125 rose to 53. This is only a little increase compared to the previous 201 count. Nothing terrible, but an ominous knock on the door.

But then in April, the news gets more disturbing; the number goes past the original high of 201, to 226.

"I don't care what you say," she says. "I think the shit just hit the fan."

"I don't agree," I reply. "It's still in a controllable area. The number isn't that much higher that last year's and he got that one down, didn't he?"

"Sure, he got it down and then the chemo ended and it's back where it is. Even higher. Where do we go from here? Back on the chemo? Or a different chemo? To a different doctor? I just don't know. I'm scared."

"I know you're scared but there's nothing to really be scared about."

"Are you scared?" she asks.

"No," I lie. I am scared to death. Decidedly, things are going badly. But I am still obsessed with the idea that I have to lie in order to protect her. I can think of no benefit to agreeing with her fears. "We're in good hands. But for now the best we can do is wait and see what happens. Maybe it'll go down again on its own."

But in May it goes to 394 and, alarmingly, to 1,839 in June. I have never heard of anyone's number going so high but the doctor is quite reassuring. He tells us that it is not unusual for it to spike upward like that from time to time and that it will probably drop again.

In mid-June she starts on a new protocol for five days, followed by another five days in Mid-July. As a result, her hair falls out once more and the CA 125 rises to 2,020. It is a life of desperation. We feel like human guinea pigs and, in many ways, Lenore certainly is a guinea pig by this time. Sometimes it feels like it might be better to just give in and stop trying, but I cannot.

Terribly discouraging. We have hoped for a return to normal, but barring that, at least a dramatic drop in the numbers. We do not anticipate a rise nor the hair loss.

This pattern continues, with the numbers relentlessly increasing each month. Her count by October is *28,000*, a number that would have been unimaginable to us earlier that year. She gets weaker and weaker and less and less hopeful. She can hardly get around unassisted and even with assistance her movements are very limited. Lenore, by now, seems to be close to dying.

Nicole wonders if this latest flare-up is related to Adam's death; that Lenore has simply unconsciously given up after that and the mind/body connection has collapsed.

The terrible responsibility to find a solution weighs on me. It is neither something I seek nor want nor agree to. It just is. I am convinced that I have no choice. But in some ways, lack of choice makes things easier. Inability to control a situation makes a person react passively. Something like being in a war and being shot at. Nothing you can do will make any difference to the outcome of the war nor your own personal outcome. When this feeling takes over, one's submission to the will of the universe results.

When Lenore became ill some of her friends were startled by my total commitment to the problem; I was startled that they were startled. While I am sure that Lenore is quite pleased with how I respond to these things, I can't imagine she is startled. Which shows she knows me and they don't.

I can see that I'm starting to feel very sorry for myself. At the same time, I think that I am not allowed to feel sorry for me instead of Lenore, who, after all, is the one who is ill. But logic has no place here. I continue to feel crushed by circumstances together with the inability to complain to anyone.

From what I learn, I determine that Herceptin is what we should be using. I know from the beginning that I am going to have a fight on my hands. Herceptin is not for ovarian cancer; it is specifically for breast cancer and not for any breast cancer but for that which has metastasized, spread. Any other cancer will be considered experimental and insurance won't pay for it.

The battle lines are drawn. No one knows if HER2 would work with Lenore and it isn't approved for ovarian regardless. Alone, I go to Dr. Patel with my story and get the anticipated objections.

"We have no reason to expect that that will work," he says. "And in any case we know nothing about HER2 with Lenore. Besides, the insurance company won't pay for it because it's not for breast cancer." Formidable argument. But I knew this going in.

"That's true enough," I reply. "But let's take the two points, one at a time. The Topotecan didn't work." (I chose not to say that she got worse on it. He knew that). "We decided not to go on the Taxotere, for reasons we discussed last time."

"And?"

"And what do you — do we — have left to try?"

"Actually, nothing."

"So this is the end of the road isn't it? What does she have to lose on Herceptin? Especially since there are no significant side effects."

"Nothing to lose. But what about the insurance company. They won't pay."

"Sure they will. She previously had breast cancer. Do you know for a fact that she doesn't still?"

"She has no symptoms."

"Can you say with certainty that there are no cancerous breast cancer cells left?"

"Of course not."

"Is it possible that the ovarian and breast cancers are related?"

"We don't know that either."

"But is it *possible?*"

"Yes. Possible."

"Then ethically you must treat both. You must give her Herceptin for the breast cancer and chemo for the ovarian."

Eventually he agrees and does as I ask. She gets Herceptin and Taxol, along with the usual retinue of Zofran, Benadryl, etc. We start on this protocol on 22 October. On 5 November her count drops from 28,000 to 22,180. Still a horrible number but a great trend. I have been telling Lenore that this will work but now I am shocked that I am right. The count on 12 November is 20,900 and then, 3 December: 14,800; 17 December: 6,580; and 23 December: 4,500.

Victory is in sight.

But it is an illusion.

". . . A RACE AGAINST TIME"

Our excitement about Nicole's pregnancy grows.

Even though Lenore recovers from the December scare, when she came close to death, in January things start to get worse again. They are not as bad as that scare, but the trend is bad.

It becomes a race against time. Will Lenore live long enough to see the baby?

Excerpt from Lenore's journal:

> *January 1999. I'm feeling sorry for myself again. A month ago my counts were dropping like a rock. Even the doctor was impressed that my numbers went down 80% in two months. Then why do I feel so bad? So tired I can hardly move. No interest in doing anything. Can't find any incentive to do anything. I feel completely wrung out.*

Huge numbers of bad things are going on.

Blood clots are a constant presence and danger. I give Lenore shots for them every day in the abdomen.

Tumors are growing in her stomach. They protrude through the skin so you can see them. It's alarming, like having an alien growing inside.

4:00 A.M. EVOLUTION OF *NOW*

The worst time is 4:00 in the morning, lying in bed, staring at the ceiling, unable to sleep, needing to sleep, and thinking. Thinking. Lying next to me, Lenore, dying. Not dying at that moment, perhaps, but dying inevitably nevertheless.

I think of Adam and what he did. And what he might have become if he had allowed me to positively influence his life more than I did. That he didn't need to die. If he were so convinced that he had no life here, that everyone knew of his past, he could have moved to California, changed his name and reinvented himself. We would have supported him in this as we did so many other things. Some, because we supported him too much, not in his best interest.

I think of him in jail with hordes of the worst the world has to offer and try to convince myself he didn't belong with them. And then Elgin State Hospital. I know that he could see only darkness in his past and his present and his future. I wonder if I would have chosen the same solution, to die. I don't know. I hope I never know. I only know he is gone and won't be back.

I think of the night he died. Instead of telling him to be quiet and go to bed, what if I had gone downstairs and talked to him? Would he still be alive? Did he die because I couldn't be bothered? I don't think so, but the image and the questions remain. I have to drag myself away from these horrors of the past and try to live in the present moment.

And I come to that present moment, here at 4:00 A.M., with my wife lying next to me. I am finally coming to terms with myself that the battle I have accepted as my own will not be won. She will die soon and I will have lost. Not only lost my partner of 35 years but lost the war that I have determined never to lose. The taste is bitter. I have tried everything I can imagine to save her but now I admit to myself that I cannot.

With failure staring me in the face, I have to do something in order to survive. One day it finally occurs to me that what is pulling me down is living in the past. I have to bring myself to the present, to the *NOW*.

Each time I think of Adam it becomes the true test of living in the *NOW*. It would have been more than easy to slip back into remembrances of previous years with him and all the misery that went with them: the drugs, alcohol, and all the other forms of anguish that rippled out. Not just for Lenore and me, but for him also. I have to virtually drag myself away from these masochistic temptations. I need to focus on the here and now and nothing else. No past. No future. Just *NOW*.

At this same time, I am not only grieving about Adam but concerned about the state of Lenore's health. Her latest bout with ovarian cancer has had me worrying on almost a daily basis, fearful she is not going to survive it, in spite of the fact I am determined she will. And Stephanie's heart condition will never get better. Will this deteriorate as we go along? Thoughts like these of what might happen in the future have as much negative power as living in the past. I can see that as destructive as it is to think of what went wrong with Adam, it is just as toxic to live in the negative future, especially since I can choose where I live at the moment. I don't have to be a passive victim, buffeted by my thoughts. So why am I *choosing* to live with thoughts of what might happen in time to come? Might. It is my choice and I am spinning out of control. I need to come back to center. The present is where the center is, not in the past or the fearful future. I add this future ingredient to my new-found view of life: living in the present, the *NOW*, not in the negative past; not in the negative future.

I think of the lessons I am teaching myself about the death of Adam. I cannot survive if I allow myself to constantly saturate my mind with thoughts and images of that final night. I am learning how to live in the present and to drop the negative past. But as I lie here in the predawn darkness I come to realize that I cannot live in this kind of present either. As I wondered if I did enough to save Adam, I now wonder if I am doing enough to save Lenore. I promoted the drug Herceptin that brought her back from the edge of death. But it was the last hope and when it failed my arsenal was depleted. I have no more. But is there one more thing that I am overlooking? Have I given up too early? I don't think so but the questions rip at me.

I make the discovery that as living is the past is destructive so is the negative present. What I have taught myself about living in the present instead of the negative past must now be expanded.

I cannot live in the negative present any more than I can live in the negative past. Instead I will find a way to live in the positive aspects of the present only.

The negative past is thinking about Adam.

The negative future is worrying what's going to happen to Stephanie.

The negative present is worrying what I am overlooking that could help Lenore. It happens less often than the other two, but at the moment it is happening, it's crushing.

I think of Stephanie and her joy in our lives. She is retarded; she has a heart that functions poorly; she is not capable of living independently. What will happen when Lenore dies? I will still be there for her but I am not Lenore. Will I take her to have her nails done every other week? Will I take her on shopping expeditions? Will I be able to defend her against the forces of the world as well as Lenore does? I think so but the questions remain. Always the questions.

I understand that I simply cannot continue to live in the negative future. I have enough to think about without having these thoughts drag me down beneath the waves. I can now see that the negative aspects of the future are as destructive as those of the past and the present. I need to add one last subject to my repertoire. In order to survive I must live in the present. At first I thought that it was the negative thoughts of Adam and his death that were swamping me. But now I can see that such thoughts from the present – the right now – and the future are just as damaging. My world needs to be pulled forward, backward and sideways into the positive present. This isn't some New Age/spiritual quest for the right way to live. It is the *only* way to live. It becomes my means of survival.

How do I handle it? A switch. Drop the negative past, future, and present. Think of all the good things in my life.

This is not a smooth transition of thought. It's a forcible wrenching. I am in quicksand right now. I'm drowning. I've got to get out of here. But I have the means to do it.

What are the means? Stop. Right now. After you say Stop, the other side of you says, Yes, but.

No *yes but*. Stop right now.

Recognize that 4 A.M. is not the time to answer valid questions, such as what is going to happen to Stephanie.

Make a commitment to yourself that at 4:00 in the *afternoon* you will think about this.

At 4 P.M.., you're going to think 'Do I even want to answer that question which isn't answerable'.

On the other hand, it is answerable: You don't have to say what terrible things are going to happen to Stephanie when Lenore dies. You can start to make a list of all the good things that will happen to her. You can plan on them.

This is the evolution and the definition of the *NOW*. It means that if the past and the future contain thoughts that are pulling you down, Stop! Right now return to the present. And if the future is comprised of negatives, Stop! Right now shift from the negative future to the positive present. Lying here in bed at four in the morning is pure torture. But it doesn't need to be. I change gears and think of the better things in my present life. About Lenore who needs me and who is grateful for what I am doing for her 24/7. About Nicole who is in the midst of her first pregnancy; and about the new baby who will be here later in the summer. About Stephanie and the delights she brings to me and those that I bring to her. My life is full of landmines, but it is surely also full of great luck and wonderful happiness. How foolish I would be if I looked on the dark side only.

I am trying to make the *NOW* an integral part of my life. It becomes very much like learning to ride a bike. I hadn't done it before but I start to become proficient. The type of bike and the tires that go on it are important as are the correct inflation of the tires, the sort of road I go on and my relationship with my bike. I learn *NOW* and feel I will never forget how to use it any more than I will forget how to ride my bike.

The subtitle of this book is Living In The *NOW*. 'Living' means just that. To *live* life in the fullest. Life is meant to be lived – not consumed by the past or the future.

"... WE ARE GOING TO LOSE"

But my new-found discovery of living in the NOW is constantly being tested.

There is a constant barrage of bad news and we have totally run out of options on chemotherapy or any other kind of therapy.

Ovarian cancer is totally taking over her body. Cancer works by grabbing some part of you and choking it off so it doesn't function anymore. Death becomes inevitable.

Being scared is cumulative. We keep piling up bad news.

At the beginning I am convinced we are going to beat it. For 18 months, I am still convinced of that. But now I finally realize that this is not going to be beatable. Somewhere in the months before she dies, Lenore knows it, too.

I also have feelings of despair. I realize we are going to lose. I feel anticipatory grief because although she hasn't died yet, I know she is going to die. The grieving process starts months before she dies.

I worry about what Stephanie is going to do without her mother. I feel I'm a good father, but it doesn't matter. Stephanie's attachment to Lenore has been incredibly different than her attachment to me.

I have a feeling of profound loss before the loss has happened. It is a terrible feeling to surrender to a loss when it's so much against your nature to give up. But you don't have a choice. This lack of choice is quite significant.

It is like if you were sent to jail and you fought it all the way with every legal appeal possible, but finally you run out of appeals and there's no use fighting anymore.

As I am doing this anticipatory grieving, I am on call 24/7 as Lenore's primary caretaker. I do everything I can to make her comfortable and to reassure her that I am there. The tough part is the perceived need on my part not to let my desperation and weariness show.

Excerpt from Lenore's journal:

And then in March, the pain started to come. It was what I dreaded the most. Dr. Patel prescribed morphine patches which I put on my arm and totally controlled the problem. In spite of the fact that I had told Jack many times that I was afraid of suffering, not dying, there was always this feeling of not knowing what was going on, and virtually living in a whirlpool. Frequently, I wanted to know exactly what was going on, and at the same time I really didn't

But the pain was a sign of things to come. I told Jack I didn't like the way this thing was going.

To my surprise he answered me frankly: 'I have to admit that things don't look good. I don't know what's causing the pain but I think we have to face up to the fact that it might be caused by tumors. In spite of the tumor-marker numbers dropping. I don't know what else it could be.'

I don't know when, but I can see the end is coming. I used to believe that I'd find some miracle that would cure everything. I don't believe that any more. Nothing is going to work.

I've decided to stop writing. I have no more energy and I can't find it in me to keep going. I've enjoyed what I've written this far but now it's time to close up shop. I'll have to leave it to others to fill in the details of the rest of my life.

By this juncture it became easier to live in the present. It was an exquisite example of how to practice it without overly trying. I think for both of us it became easier doing it together because we had been doing it in smaller ways for some time. Then, when we needed it, it was there for us. No longer any point in thinking about the past or the future. It all became meaningless. Lenore's deteriorating condition took over both our lives and the fifteen minute radius in which we were caught up totally captured us. Nothing existed except that which was happening right now. The idea that tomorrow might not happen for Lenore wasn't a necessary part of our thoughts. It presented itself in her actions and reactions without thinking it out. We lived from day to day. Every small time we could think of something to do together, we did it, and treasured the moment.

✢

END IN SIGHT

CONFRONTING PAIN

At the beginning of April Lenore is using the maximum strength lollipops, but the pain has outstripped the patches and the lollipops. Something more serious is needed. Morphine pills, called MSIR, are prescribed. This is the serious drug we are looking for.

I certainly don't trust letting Lenore self-medicate and I am too neurotic on the subject to even dream of allowing anyone else to supervise. The result is that in trusting only myself, I rarely leave the house. I go out only to get food and prescriptions. Whenever I am out, I am plagued with the thought that I ought not to be wherever I am, that I am needed at home. Life outside the house becomes nerve-wracking.

Medications are required 16 hours a day, every day. I have to pay close attention to the time so as not to forget the right thing at the right time. As with the Lovenox, I have to negotiate with Lenore each time I give her all the other meds.

I never tell her so, but I enjoy her participation. If she knows I am on to her, it will spoil the whole thing and take away her feeling of ownership.

Lenore's CA 125 had been falling and reached a low of 4,500 at the end of December. But now, three months later, the numbers confirm what we have known for some time. The pain and the visibility of the tumors are followed by the latest reading: 7,556. The handwriting on the wall can no longer be denied or ignored. Now, in April, we are entering a stage where we haven't been before. There is no more research to be done; no options to be tried, except drug trials in which one is essentially a research subject with unknown side effects.

"The time has come," Lenore said, "to see where we go from here. I'm still on the Herceptin and the chemo, and the count and tumors are both growing. What do you think we should do?"

"I know what I think we should do," I reply, "but I'd rather wait for your input. What do you think?"

"I want to stop the chemo. I see no reason to keep it up. It is giving me false hope, but now it's not even doing that. I'm fresh out of hope."

"I think you're right, but I wanted you to come to that conclusion without my influence. We're partners in this, but that one's just too personal."

"Would you call Dr. Patel and tell him?"

"Now?"

"Yeah. I'd like to get it behind me."

I call him and he agrees without dispute or discussion. I imagine he thinks we should have done this before now, but like me, doesn't want to be the one to pull the plug, so to speak.

When I hang up, Lenore says, "I feel like celebrating. Let's call Rosum and invite her to dinner. Tell her we're celebrating, but don't tell her what."

I call Rosum and she agrees to meet us but really pushes to know what the occasion is. I won't tell her. We meet at the Good Life Café, a restaurant we all like. Now, Lenore and I take pleasure in the dark humor of the name.

"Happy Birthday," we say.

"Okay, since it's not my birthday, what is it you two are so happy about?"

"I stopped chemo today," Lenore says. "We're celebrating."

Rosum's half smile betrays her inability to digest this. I suppose she realizes that Lenore isn't kidding but doesn't think it can be good news.

A week later, I am walking with Lenore to the bathroom when she staggers but doesn't fall. She is getting weaker and of course knows it. I notice she is getting quite thoughtful.

The next day she says, "I need your help."

"Of course," I answer. "In what?"

"You promised me that I won't suffer. I want you to help me when the time comes. You know, to help me get out of here."

"You mean commit suicide?"

"Yes."

"I think you're a bit premature." I say.

"I know that. But I want you to promise me that when the time comes you'll be there for me and not chicken out."

"I told you I would and I will."

"How will you do it?" she asks.

I haven't expected this question and I admit it. "I have no idea. But I'll find out."

"How?"

"I don't know. I'll get a book on the subject.

Lenore never again refers to suicide, secure in the knowledge that everything is in place for what she wants, should she need it.

I am happy that she has no idea of my doubts that I could do anything to help her.

This section emphasizes giving up unintentional false hope. Thinking that there was a cure, in effect, would have given false hope when there was no hope. The 'right' drug doesn't exist and thinking it might, becomes a false hope. Thankfully, living in the *NOW* does not include this false hope. Addressing reality allowed Lenore and me to live in the *present*, and living there became a freeing thing for both of us. We found the ability to celebrate in just being together.

We no longer needed to live in a land where reality no longer existed. Finding the boundary between hope and reality, however, is a tricky game. You don't want to leave hope behind too soon, nor do you want to hold onto it when it no longer exists. If you have to err, do it on the side of hope. But then, on the day it leaves, let it go, gracefully and with gratitude that it served you when it needed to.

HOSPICE

Asleep and awake begin to merge. Lenore drifts off to sleep, sometimes in the midst of a conversation and then awakens, not knowing she has left. Generally she sleeps all night, but the days are harder to define because of erratic sleeping patterns. Part of this is the morphine, but other parts are the physical and mental stresses of the disease.

When she is awake I am there, but when she is asleep I go downstairs. Because I have no way of knowing when she wakes up, we devise a system to let me know. We have two phone lines and whenever she wants to reach me, she simply calls on the second line and I came back upstairs. This provides her with a good feeling of security. It also does the same for me, doing away with my apprehension that she is awake without me knowing it. But I also have a cell phone for those times when I go to the store.

At about this time our daughter, Stephanie, begins to have more difficulties with breathing due to her heart condition. She has to have a phlebotomy every six weeks, having blood drawn in order to decrease the volume in her arteries. This has the effect of thinning her blood, (which at times gets almost as thick as molasses, due to too much hemoglobin), thereby decreasing her chance of having a stroke. Nevertheless, even though her condition has been with her since birth, she is getting noticeably less able to walk any distance without having shortness of breath. It got to the point that if Lenore and Rosemary went shopping with Stephanie, they had to bring her wheelchair along in order not to worry about her. As Lenore's condition deteriorates, it almost seems like a tossup as to who needs the chair more.

Stephanie's cardiologist recommends that she be put on oxygen for about four to six hours a day. The problem with that is her place of residence, Riverside Foundation, is not licensed to have oxygen. This is a silly rule since the oxygen that would be given to her would be drawn from the air, not from a tank and therefore poses no threat to the facility. Oxygen in a tank is highly compressed and is flammable; the oxygen for Stephanie comes from a portable machine which separates it from the air and is not compressed; it is therefore not flammable.

However, as we all know, there is no point in trying to point out logic to a bureaucracy and Riverside would lose the battle to the State even before it had begun. My solution is to bring her home every day, seven days a week, for six hours. She sits in the office in the front part of the house, which is on the ground floor so that she doesn't have to climb stairs. I get the machine from a medical supply company and she sits watching soap operas, eating lunch, and generally having a good time with it.

Riverside has a workshop where the residents spend five days a week and Stephanie is frequently bored with it. This opportunity to come home for oxygen therapy is a welcome respite for her. The add-on of soap operas is more than she could have hoped for.

At this point Hospice enters our lives.

"Sooner or later we're going to have to get you more personalized medical attention," I say.

"What does more personalized mean?" Lenore asks.

"It's too tough for you to get to Dr. Patel's. I mean you are still going there, but you need to be going more than you used to and it's getting tougher each trip. We need to have someone come here so you don't have to go there."

"How do we do that? Like who?"

"Well, there's different ways of doing it."

"Like what?" she asks.

"I don't know. I have to check into it further."

"I don't believe you," she replies. "You've already checked into it. What aren't you telling me?"

I am very uncomfortable with her questions. I want to control the conversation and lead it in the direction of my choice when I want to. But she isn't letting me. Lenore is requiring more serious meds and ever more frequent medical attention, yet her ability to get to the doctor's office is decreasing. I have to do something different.

"Nothing," I say. "I think we need to have something like home health care. Someone to come here for you."

"Why are you beating around the bush? Who are you thinking of?"

"I'm thinking of hospice," I reply. Now the cat is out of the bag.

"You make it sound as if you're apologizing. What's wrong with hospice? Aren't they home health care?"

"Yeah, but they have some requirements." She looks at me, as if asking what they were.

"One of the requirements is that you can't be on any meds that are designed to help you get well," I say. I would rather have a tooth pulled than continue with this conversation.

"Well, I'm not, am I? What am I taking that would be a problem?"

"Nothing. Only pain killers."

"So that's not a problem, is it?" she asks. "What's the real problem?"

"The second requirement." I don't know how to get out of it now. "You have to decide that you're not going to live a lot longer for hospice to get involved." Actually, it goes even a step further than that. We have to get a note from her doctor saying that she isn't expected to live more than another six months. I don't have the heart to tell her that part.

"I don't have a problem with that," she says. "There's no way I'm going to live a lot longer. What do you think?"

"I think that as long as we're able to tell them that, then we're ok. I didn't know if you are comfortable with it."

"I'm not comfortable with the idea of dying, but I know where I am. I know that I'm going to die, but I don't know

when. I know I won't be here next year, but I do want to hang
on for Nicole's baby. I don't know if that's possible."

"Of course it's possible," I reply. But that is four months
away and I don't believe it is possible. Sometimes it's a curse
to understand too much.

"Well, if you want to try out hospice, it's ok with me. Do
you know who to talk to?"

"I'll ask Dr. Patel." The fact is that I have already talked
to him and gotten the phone number of *Hospice of the North
Shore* in a northern suburb of Chicago. However, I wait to call
them until I talk it over with Lenore.

When I do call, I am put in touch with one of a number
of people who are to be our lifesavers. Lenore's primary nurse
will be Vicki Chandler. She is eminently suited for her job —
a caring, loving, beautiful human being with an accent that
comes from somewhere south of Chicago. She is plump, with a
face straight from a Norman Rockwell calendar, like someone
ready to help carve the turkey.

It is a privilege to meet her and the rest of her crew: Catherine Oberlander, Debbie Lee, and the wonderful Gloria May,
who bathes Lenore and returns to her some quality of life.
These are people who are invariably cheerful in spite of the
certain knowledge that 100% of their patients will die.

Vicki brings with her a supply of the MSIR morphine pills
and, when these became less effective, switches them to a liq-
uid form. From then on she simply phones in a prescription
and the meds are delivered by a pharmacy that is in close touch
with Hospice.

The routine works well: three times a week, with seven-
day availability, Vicki or one of the other nurses come to the
house to monitor the pain medications. Twice a week Gloria
comes and gives Lenore a bath right in her bed. She loves it.

Lenore, of course, is getting weaker by the day. She needs
my help to get to the bathroom, then regresses from that to
needing a walker to support herself. Eventually she requires
a commode next to her bed because she can't even use the

walker. All this time, her constipation increases due to the morphine on one hand and to an obstructed bowel on the other. We have been warned that this is a possibility, but until it happens, there is no way to understand how miserable it really is. In order for her to find some measure of comfort, I give her enemas daily, sometimes twice a day.

Rosum takes a week's vacation and comes over every day, remaining the great friend she has always been. This enables Lenore to live in the *NOW*, because of the presence of friends and caring people.

On May 2nd we make what seems to be just another routine visit to Dr. Patel. It proves to be our last time. We go because of her ever-worsening constipation. The only way I am able to get her there is by using the wheelchair. I still don't remember how I got her downstairs. Rosemary recalls that I carried her. The doctor feels that the constipation will be self-limiting. I want her to go to the hospital to have the problem resolved by mechanical rather than pharmaceutical means. He doesn't agree, but without being specific as to why. I think he feels the stress might kill her. I feel the chance of relieving the pain and discomfort is worth the risk at this point. We had reached a crossroad with little to lose as long as we keep her comfortable. This is true of so many things in life: the crossroads are there frequently; it is up to us to recognize and act on them.

Control what you can. Let go of what you cannot.

I couldn't change the course of Lenore's illness, but I could help her to be as comfortable as possible each day. Focusing on the *NOW* let us both relish her pleasure in the baths she got from hospice, and let her choose not to dwell on the worries about her future.

At first, I was more concerned about her future than she was. But she was able to let go of the fear of the future and accept the inevitable that was. When I realized this in her, she inadvertently allowed me to come back to living in the present, the *NOW*, with her. There was no need to live in the past, thinking of all the grief that had brought us to that moment;

and there certainly was no logic in living in the negative future. Especially after I got her permission not to do so.

I was also able to improve the quality of Stephanie's life in two ways — getting her the oxygen she needed and giving her a great experience watching soap operas. I could not change her underlying heart condition, but I could make her *NOW* a time of happy mornings and afternoons. The present time she lived in was as close to heaven as is possible to achieve.

END GAME

The temperature in the bedroom is above freezing, but not much higher. The air conditioner is at full blast because Lenore vacillates between being too hot and too cold. Unfortunately, when she is too cold, she wraps herself in a heavy comforter on the bed, leaving only her head sticking out, but still wants the AC left on. Everyone who comes into the room treats this as if it were quite normal. Two of her friends, Ginger and Carol, come over and have to sit in side chairs enclosed in blankets, all the while denying that they are cold. It is goofy, but it has the desired effect.

When we are able to slide the temperature up to something resembling normal, they bring in food. Lenore eats either in place in bed or sits on the end of the bed with a card table pulled in close, with the rest of us at the same table or in scattered chairs around the room. The food is good, wine flows and the *joie de vivre* is surprisingly high.

Occasions such as this naturally become rarer as April comes to an end. A lot of Lenore's weakness is due to not eating at all. The disease is robbing her of interest.

Occasionally, breathing becomes difficult for her, and she finds comfort in using oxygen which is already available. Stephanie's machine is in the office directly below the bedroom. It has a thin hose which must be fifty feet long with a device on the end which loops over the ears and then to the nostrils where two prongs send oxygen in. I turn on the machine and then take the coiled hose with me as I walk up the stairs, around the corner, and into the bedroom. Strangely enough, during this time Stephanie expresses less interest in visiting her mother upstairs, saying in her usual diplomatic way that she would love to see her, but just not at this time.

Lenore's pain increases somewhat and the hospice nurses change the type of medication to MS Contin, a powerful pain-killer. This still tends to cause constipation, but because she isn't eating as often, the problem lessens.

Lenore's brother Norman arrives on May 3rd and stays for a week. He is well aware of the fragile state of his sister's health and is understandably torn about coming. He wants to be there, knowing it will be the last time he will see her alive. But he also doesn't want to be there for exactly the same reason. It is difficult for him to cope with the reality of unpleasant situations.

Once more her medication needs an upgrade for pain control. A morphine pump is the solution.

She rarely eats by this time, and her general state of being is near collapse.

Norman's former wife, Pam, comes on the 20th for three days. She and Lenore are very close and it is tough for her to come. To discover her ability to be with Lenore severely limited must make her wonder if she has chosen wisely. I feel, though, that she knew the situation before leaving California and made the decision that she wants to see Lenore before she dies instead of using her limited funds to go to her funeral.

The end game is finally here. I suppose we all know it, but no one says it.

Knowing that the end is approaching does nothing to lessen the emotional impact. But being worn down day after day takes its toll, and eventually both the patient and the care-giver have suffered enough grief and a numbness settles in. The desire to win this game lessens, but strangely enough doesn't leave, when acceptance of inevitable defeat is finally reached. Preparations for the end are put in place, and when this happens a sort of peace takes over, knowing that everything that needs to be done has been done.

It is a ritual, a dance that most of us must go thru sooner or later; but still, when it comes time to enter it, it comes as a surprise as if ours was the first time. Lenore is at peace with her dying and her siblings relatives and friends find that they also have enough time to say what they need to say. It is all quite civilized.

END

We rent a movie from Blockbuster called 'Apt Pupil'. Nicole and Larry come over on a Friday night and we put it on the VCR in our bedroom. It is about a former Nazi who had successfully assimilated himself in this country and then his secret is discovered by a boy. After watching it for a half hour, Lenore asks if we would turn it off because she is tired. Instead of viewing it in another room, we decide to wait to watch it until the next night, Saturday, the 29th of May. During that day Nicole and Larry stay with Lenore while I run a number of errands. One them is to go to a funeral home near the house and arrange for Lenore's funeral. This gives me an eerie sense of *déjà vu;* I had done this same thing 21 years previously as my father lay dying. I don't want to have to make these arrangements after she has died and, since her death seems imminent, it is foolish not to make them now. I arrange to have her cremated, as was Adam almost a year and a half before, and the ceremony will be in the same funeral building.

Stephanie has come over that morning and, as usual, gets her oxygen therapy in the main floor office of the house. At about noon, one of the hospice nurses, Catherine Oberlander, comes over and is seeing to Lenore. Stephanie is in the kitchen, trailing her lengthy oxygen hose behind, with the surplus coiled over one arm. I am standing in the front hall with Catherine when Stephanie comes around the corner and says, "Could I please go upstairs and see Mom?" I am startled, since she has avoided doing so for the past few weeks. But I am delighted and help her slowly make the climb. She goes into the bedroom, sits on a side chair, and the two of them have a lengthy chat. It isn't hard to imagine that this really makes Lenore's day. Shortly after I take Stephanie back to Riverside, where she lives.

That evening the three of us make sure Lenore is comfortable in bed, and then go downstairs to finish "Apt Pupil". Lenore sleeps on an air mattress in the bed supplied by hospice. It has a sort of waffle design on top, made to prevent bed sores for a person who is spending quite of bit of time there. Freshly bathed by Gloria, and in a clean night shirt, she is as comfortable as is possible under the circumstances; the morphine pump is keeping her in a zone of comfort between no pain and no stress.

About halfway through the film, I decide to go upstairs to see how she is doing, although there really is no need since she is most probably sleeping. As I walk into the bedroom, my eyes dart from the bed *which is empty*, to the floor next to it, which is where Lenore is lying, face up, looking as if she belonged there. Trying not to show panic in my voice, I say, "Hi, how are you doing?" By then I am standing over her, looking straight down.

"Fine," she replies. "What are you guys doing?"

"Oh, we're all downstairs watching that movie we started. Remember? The one you didn't like?"

"No," she said, "I don't recall. But I can't remember every movie I've seen lately. Do you like it?"

"Oh, it's all right. I've seen better. Why are you lying on the floor, by the way?"

She looks puzzled for a moment and then seems to notice for the first time that she isn't in bed. "I don't know," she says. "I must have gotten out of bed to go to the john and slipped down. God, it's getting terrible. You know, to fall out of bed and not even know you're out of bed." She laughs at this.

"I don't think it's so terrible. A lot of people do that. I did it myself once or twice." I hope she doesn't have a follow-up question for that one. She doesn't. She just nods slightly.

I say, "Hold on a minute. I have to ask Larry something."

I go outside the bedroom door and call Larry in a hoarse whisper to come upstairs. When he gets there he looks understandably startled to see Lenore on the floor, but I put my finger to my lips so that he won't say anything. I imagine he won't, but can't take the chance. I ask him to go all the way to the other side of the bed and then lie across it so that he is then looking down on Lenore from the bed. I pick her up and after I place her back in bed, Larry pulls on the sheet which covers the air mattress in order to position her correctly, sort of like pulling on a tablecloth while the food is still on the table. When we get her where we want her, I put her sheet and blanket back over her and go to bed myself. Even though she theoretically can't get out of bed, if she did it once she somehow might do it again. I lie there unable to sleep, thinking that every little noise is her trying once more to leave. It seems as if I don't sleep all night, but I assume I drift off here and there before frequently being jolted back awake.

Nicole and Larry intended to go back home that Saturday night, but after the bed incident, decide to sleep over.

At about 6:30 in the morning Lenore says, "Could I have some orange juice? With lots of ice?"

I go downstairs and get a large glass filled with ice before filling it with juice. I also get a second glass and fill it with juice alone for refills. I keep thinking what a demeaning situation Lenore finds herself in. I beat up on myself once more for not having the courage to help put her out of her misery. I think of the movie, "They Shoot Horses, Don't They?" But whenever I let my brain come up for air, I realize that she isn't in misery, and, as demeaning as I think her situation is, I have no idea what she thinks. For all I know, she isn't on the same track as me. After all, she hasn't brought up the subject in a while; certainly not since she got into dire straits. But logic isn't a necessary antidote for me keeping up the drumbeat on myself. I give her a few more of her morning meds. She takes them with the orange juice, this time without negotiating.

Then I get in bed and lie next to her and we talk. She dozes off briefly a few times and when she wakes back up, we talk some more as if she hadn't left. She starts to say something, pauses and says, "I love you, Jack."

"I love you too," I reply. These were the last words we are to speak to each other. If I had written the script, they would have been exactly those, no more and no less. At about 8:00 she falls asleep again, but this time I notice her breathing is somewhat irregular and that her eyes are slightly open. Still lying next to her, I stroke her arm and speak to her softly. I realize she has probably slipped into a coma, but I remember that people in comas frequently can hear what's going on around them.

Nicole and Larry come into the room from time to time and leave again. At about 9:15 Nicole comes back alone and sits at the furthest corner of the bed. I go over and sit next to her. Quietly, I say, "Do you know what's happening?" looking back at Lenore.

"No," she says, "do you?"

I have never seen anyone die before, but now my instinct is talking to me.

"I think so," I say.

She realizes what I am saying and says, "Do you think you should call Rosum? And Helene?"

"Yes. I'll call from another room."

I go down the hall and call them both. My conversation in each case is brief and identical: "Hi. I think it would be a good idea if you come right over."

"Right now?"

"Yes, right now."

"Okay. Thanks."

I go back to the bedroom as Larry walks in and Nicole is walking out, crying to herself. I lie down again next to Lenore and resume stroking her arm and talking to her. I think to myself that Adam also died on a Sunday morning. At about 9:30 her breathing becomes noticeably more labored and even stops and starts. I speak softly to her and tell her that if she needs to leave it is all right to let go. She stops breathing. For a while I'm not sure what has happened. But then I know. I go around to her side of the bed and kiss her. Then I go down the hall and tell Nicole.

Fifteen minutes later, I look out the window and see Rosum arrive, followed a minute later by Helene. Both are standing on the lawn talking to Nicole and all three are crying. Rosum is the first to come upstairs and stand in the doorway, asking if it is all right to come in. I tell her of course it is all right, and then say that she would probably like some private time with Lenore. She asks if she could touch Lenore and I say yes. I leave and close the door behind me. A while later, she emerges from the room, crying. This was repeated with Helene.

I call Hospice. In less than an hour a nurse comes and takes charge of the scene. She removes all the meds from the room and, in accordance with their rules, flushes them down the toilet. She then asks us to leave the room. After closing the door, she bathes Lenore and changes her clothes into another night shirt, fluffs her pillow, and straightens out the blanket. When we come back into the room it is exactly the same as if she is sleeping peacefully.

I ask Helene and Rosum to phone everyone they feel appropriate and I call the funeral home, asking them to come over, but not until about noon. I simply don't want her whisked out of the house. I want whoever comes over to be able to visit her in the surroundings she loved so much. When the people from the funeral home finally do come, I tell them I want them to take her out with her face uncovered. I want her to leave with dignity.

The funeral is to be three days later on Wednesday, June 2nd. I don't immediately tell Stephanie that her mother has died, mostly because I don't know what else to do. So the day Lenore dies, I tell her that Lenore is in Florida in a hospital and is *very* ill. The next day I tell her that Lenore is getting sicker and there is a strong chance she might die. On Tuesday I finally tell her that Lenore has died and that the funeral is to be the next day. Thus prepared over the course of days and comforted by her coterie of friends at Riverside, she is able to cope with the loss very well. She sits in the front row at the funeral with me, Nicole and Larry, and with one of her friends on each side.

We arrange for a service almost identical with Adam's, except that we have a rabbi conducting. Lenore has been cremated and the bronze urn is on a draped side table surrounded by numerous photographs documenting the various stages of her life with her friends and family. As with Adam, her friends and relatives speak about her in their own words, most more moving than anything written by a professional.

Until you have been connected closely to someone who has been dying over a period of time, it seems that the death is the ordeal, but death is the easiest part of the ordeal. The months, if not years, leading up to the final event, comprise the true suffering. For whom, you might ask, the patient or the survivors? And the answer is yes.

The service was almost identical with Adam's, but the similarities end there. Adam chose to die; Lenore did not. Adam's death was a sudden shock, abrupt but not totally unexpected, considering his history with drugs, depression and alcohol. But with Lenore death was a long time coming. The abruptness wasn't there. For those two years there were 'little deaths' on an ongoing basis almost weekly. She and I died in small pieces; she physically; I, down in the inner emotional core of my being.

It is wearing physically – time to do something else. Doing it, failing. Always failing.

Failing. This is the feeling that I have. But failing is a poor word for that situation. It is totally beyond my control, beyond the control of the medical community as a whole.

I keep taking it personally. Maybe because Lenore expected I'll come up with a solution. Not at the end, but during the first 18 months of her illness.

Dying over an extended period of time produces what could be called anticipatory grieving. The grieving over anticipated death begins long before someone dies and lasts after death occurs. This type of grieving cannot be compared with grieving from a sudden loss; by its nature, much of the grieving has been done over time. As each day goes by a little more grief enters the world of the family and friends of the person dying. As such it is no different in its intensity than that coming from sudden death, but because it is portioned out, one has the ability to experience it every day in what I described above as 'little deaths, weekly'.

Allowing oneself to grieve has already happened in great part, even though the closure needed by the death itself still lies in the immediate future. The anticipatory grieving has been extensive. Part of anticipatory grief – making, using and cementing connections with others – has already been done, and you will eventually find comfort in the fact that you will once more be able to re-enter the world — albeit the *modified* world — you once knew.

STEPHANIE

I feel quite sorry for myself having to deal with replacing Lenore as far as Stephanie is concerned. I don't feel I am up to succeeding at it. I can't be the lioness that Lenore was.

This whole victim feeling is totally internalized. There is no one to whom I can tell I feel like a victim. Besides, I hate the feeling. I am simply sorry for myself.

It is hard coming back to earth. After months of being chief nurse and having my days and nights consumed by this, overnight I am faced with having nothing to do. For weeks I am uneasy being in a store very long, convinced that I shouldn't be there. That I am needed at home. Even when logic intervenes, I remain unsettled.

Immediately after Lenore died, I was totally occupied with the events that attend a funeral. But now, the people have left, the tasks are all done, and everything is past tense. Except me. I need to reorganize my life and to devote more time to Stephanie. Not that she feels neglected. With her circle of friends at Riverside, she is able to cope quite well. She finds the constant attention she receives from both residents and staff to be both welcome and flattering.

In addition to Stephanie coming to my house five days a week for oxygen therapy, I am still taking her to have blood drawn, a phlebotomy, every six weeks. She hates the insertion of the needle at the blood lab, but loves the people there at Northwestern Hospital. By this time, she has been going for years. She knows them and they know her by name, making her feel like a pampered princess, getting her orange juice, cookies, and warm blankets.

Her cardiologist is also at Northwestern, though in another building in the vast complex. Whenever she goes she gets the absolute best of care, not only from Dr. McPherson, who is voted by his peers as best in the city for echocardiograms, but from the other eminent heart specialists who specialize in congenital defects.

Even with the best care in the world, however, it is apparent that she is slowly but surely declining. She was born with three heart defects which could not be corrected, and so interdependent that if one were repaired surgically, the others would kill her. She could get worse, but she could not get better. As her need for oxygen therapy grows, so does her joy for life. One thing can be said for Stephanie, she leads a good and fruitful life, every day.

In early August, her sister Nicole is about to give birth. Stephanie can hardly contain herself. She realizes that she cannot have babies, though not why. But she awaits her niece or nephew with joy. We are hoping that the baby would make an appearance on the 4th or 6th, Stephanie's and Nicole's birthdays, but it doesn't happen. The wonder boy Jamie is born on the 12th, but not without complications. He is to remain in the hospital for 10 days, due to a blood disorder having to do with an antibody conflict between Nicole and Larry's blood. It is very distressing for all of us, but Stephanie is mercifully unaware of the situation. I bring her to the hospital to visit Jamie and she is able to rub his cheek but not hold him. She pulls her wheelchair as close as possible to his crib in ICU and never stops staring at him with love in her eyes.

As usual I am concerned with her lack of ability to walk very far, but she has dodged so many bullets in all her years that this is just one more.

On Thursday, the 19th she goes to see Dr. McPherson for an Echo. Again, it turns out perfectly acceptable, given the circumstances. We have our discussion with the cardiologists afterward and go out for dinner, which is Stephanie's favorite sport.

On Sunday evening, the 22nd, I get a call from Riverside saying that Stephanie is feeling lightheaded and that as a precaution they have her taken to Condell Hospital. I go there at about 9:00 and have no trouble finding her in the ER. I simply follow the sound of giggles coming from one of the draped areas. She is sitting up in bed with a nurse on one side and a staff member from Riverside on the other. In the brief time it takes me to get there, they have already attached an oxygen mask to her face, drawn blood, and inserted an IV. There is really nothing effective they can do for her, but when faced with such a situation a hospital will perform tests. Part of their reasoning, I suppose, is because if they don't, someone will sue them. While this is understandable, it leaves the patient suffering through the tangles that result. Stephanie stays there while we wait for 'results' and for various hospital people to talk to her. They have no idea why she is still there, but as long as no one gives official permission for her to leave, they want her to stay. Finally at 3:00 in the morning, exasperated, I tell them I am checking her out. I am told that it would have to be *AMA*: Against Medical Advice. I suppose that this is intended to scare me into leaving her there, but I am well beyond that. I return her to Riverside and am amazed to find that her roommate Laura is sitting up in bed, waiting for her. She won't admit she is worried, but as soon as Stephanie arrives, she goes to sleep. I leave, smiling.

The next night is like a repeat of the first. I get a call from Riverside saying that Stephanie is feeling logy and that they are about to call an ambulance to take her back to the hospital. I tell them to leave her where she is and that I will be right over. They probably assume I will be taking her to Condell myself. I grab a tank of oxygen from my front office (in addition to the oxygen machine, I have two tanks on hand), which is on a two-wheel cart, and zip over to see what is going on. When I arrive, she is in her room in a wheelchair. Her head had been lolling against her shoulder and she is virtually unresponsive. In one motion, I put an oxygen mask over her face and turn on the tank. Within a few minutes of the infusion of oxygen, she starts to perk up and the color returns to her face. Within ten minutes of my arrival, she is back to her old self. I stay for about an hour, at which time I say I am taking her home to my house. The staff becomes visibly nervous, saying that they think she should go to the hospital. I explain that the only thing they will do for her is give her oxygen and stick needles in her. I can do the same minus the needles. I leave and take her home.

In my office, there is a white sofa which converts to a double bed. I make this up and put her to bed, still with the mask on her. I then crawl in to the other half of the bed and we talk for a while. Eventually she asks if she could sleep without the mask and I agree. I am somewhat nervous with what is happening, but once more revert to the bullet-dodging theory and I stay with her.

At 5:00 in the morning, she gets up to go to the john and when she returns she starts to get back in, but instead falls face forward into her side of the bed. I quickly get the oxygen mask and put it on her. She immediately revives and says, "Daddy, I'm *scared*."

So am I but I say, "Steph, this has happened before, hasn't it?"

"Yes, Daddy."

"And it always turned out ok each time, didn't it?"

"Yes, Daddy."

"Well this is no different than those other times. I know it's scary, but everything's going to be all right."

"Okay, Daddy, if you say so."

"So lie back down and go to sleep."

I decide to call 911, but choose to leave the room to do it for fear of making her nervous. The paramedics arrive shortly, arriving in a fire truck and an ambulance. They bundle her up in a sort of sit up stretcher and take her off to the hospital. Her eyes are shut and I can't tell if she is just closing them or if she is sleeping or possibly unconscious. I ask if they could take her downtown to Northwestern Hospital, but they say they are obliged to take her to the closest hospital, Northwest Community. As they leave I plan out the day in my head: After she stabilizes at the hospital I will order another ambulance and take her downtown to Northwestern and her cardiologist. This could easily take the entire day, so I take the dogs outside and then feed them, not knowing when they would see me again. I leave for Northwest Community and when I arrive I go to the ER to find her.

I hear giggles coming from one of the curtained areas, but when I look in it isn't her. I stop a nurse and ask if she knows where she is. She doesn't recognize the name, but just then a second nurse, hearing Stephanie's name says, "Hold on, I'll take care of it." She goes around a corner and a little while later a man in a light gray suit and a clerical collar comes up to me and introduces himself.

"Are you Stephanie's dad?" he asks.

"Yes, I am. Do you know where she is?" I reply.

"I'm sorry, Mr. Cain, but Stephanie didn't make it. She passed away on the way to the hospital."

It is exactly as if I have physically walked into a brick wall. I can feel the impact and then immediately I feel numb. I know what he is saying but can't absorb it. It is too terrible to be real.

I follow him to the far end of the ER, aware somehow that the staff is glancing at me as I pass. He pulls back the drape at the last cubicle. There is Stephanie lying on a bed with her eyes closed. I sit next to her on a three-legged stool and break down as the cleric leaves me alone. I have no idea how long I am there, but when I am finally able to collect myself I walk out. He escorts me to a small room off the ER where there is a table with a phone next to two sofas.

I call Nicole first. I feel sorry for her and sorry for myself to have to be the one to deliver the shock of her second, and last, sibling's death. I call Helene and Rosum and ask them to call others as they see fit, including Riverside. Even though my car is at the hospital, I am not able to drive. Helene's husband kindly comes to the hospital to drive me home.

Stephanie's funeral a few days later is attended by about 30 Riverside residents and an overflow crowd which requires opening the wall of an adjoining room, which is still inadequate. Her best friends Laura and Gigi sit in the front with me, near two easels of photographs on either side of the cremation urn.

The same rabbi who conducted Lenore's funeral conducts Stephanie's. I had asked him previously if he would use the same wording for the 23rd Psalm as was done for Adam, changing the 'my' to 'you'. For instance, "The Lord is your shepherd, you shall not want, etc." But the rabbi firmly refused, saying that he would not revise Scripture. And so, he read the 23rd Psalm at both Lenore's and Stephanie's in the same, 'original' text.

In a subsequent conversation, the rabbi encourages me to read the Book of Job in the Bible, saying that I would gain comfort from it. On the contrary. I have never read it before, but I think it is disturbing that God would virtually conspire with the Devil to visit plague after plague upon Job, who had done nothing up until that time but serve God nobly. God's supposed reason for doing this was to demonstrate to the Devil that no matter what he deliberately did to Job, Job would not desert God. I think that if Job had simply endured misfortune, *without God's participating in Job's misery*, and still remained faithful to God, it might have been inspiring. Instead it makes me feel anything but comforted reading it. I can't imagine what message the rabbi gained from it.

✦

COMING BACK

THE ROAD TO RECOVERY

It feels like the day after the war ended. The battles were long and bloody, but now they're behind me and there's nothing more I have to do. I feel irrelevant. I was necessary when I was needed, but there's no one left standing except Nicole and me. The sudden stop after these years of being the strength of others is jarring in the silence. Some part of me wants to move on with my life but that's my rational/logical side. My emotional side wins, and I have no interest in moving on. I am too overwhelmed with feeling sorry for myself to move on.

I was still consumed with grief for Adam when Lenore died, and then barely had time to absorb Lenore's death when, less than three months later, Stephanie followed. Along the way, I learn something about grief. There's no such thing as one-dimensional grief. I thought the grief I felt for Adam was what it was all about. But mine was the emotional response to suicide. Not the same as the sudden death from a heart attack. Certainly not the same as the long trial of death from cancer.

When I think about my response to the suicide, the closest feeling I can describe is the suddenness of heart failure combined with the insult of a permanent slap in the face. This is followed by grief alternating with anger. Desperately trying to forgive Adam for what he did to me, ignoring what he did to

the rest of the family, not to say himself. I am taking it personally, although illogically. While the grief is obvious, the anger
is not, coming as it is from the frustration that I am helpless.
There's nothing I can do. He's already dead. And so I rage
against the injustice perpetrated against me. Me. I have no
use for his possible reason nor his state of mind. I am much
too self-absorbed in the grief that is coming at me, and that I
cannot deflect.

And now this profound sorrow with its mixture of anger
is threatening to consume me. I cannot forgive him, and I cannot forgive myself for not forgiving him. I am crushed by the
weight of what I am doing.

When Lenore dies, I learn that another kind of grief alto-
gether has come into my life. She — and I — had been battling
her cancer for years and now we have lost. Always knowing
that losing was at the end of our trail doesn't make the pain
any less searing. I have convinced myself that we — I — would
beat this thing, at least until near the end, when reality brings
me back.

Grief has already been preceded by anticipatory grief,
triggered at first by the results that I demanded—and didn't
receive—of the chemo, and eventually by the obvious signs
of imminent defeat. Now the combat is over and my partner
of 35 years is dead. I am already worn thin, but am still beset
by the mental wailing of a Job. Not being able to summon
even the illogic of anger, I am left with the self-immolation of
my soul. Because Nicole has her own burden, I cannot bring
myself to tell her of my tribulations. I am quite alone. I don't
know where to turn.

Before I am able to come to terms with this dilemma,
Stephanie dies. A totally different type of grief swallows me.
No suicide here and no anger is possible. A weak heart has
brought her down. But the suddenness of her death devas-
tates me. We all knew it was coming for years, but I refused
to see it. I am overcome with grief so paralyzing that I am
barely able to function. I cannot stop thinking of her lying

behind the curtained area in the ER. I have no more *NOW* left to help me.

And here I am, left to my own devices. I have nothing left to do with my life and no interest in doing anything. Three key components of my life have left in an unreasonably short period of time, leaving me with a vacancy in my heart and my mind. I have no interest in changing this. My self pity is so intense that I have no room for reasonable thinking. Quite honestly, I have no interest in thinking, logical or otherwise. I prefer to be controlled by my grief, and the fact that I have no choice is strangely comforting. I am not able to make decisions, nor is anyone expecting that I should do so. I feel entitled to being in my victim mode.

There's a feeling at this point, that having battled one disaster after another, it's all over. I've survived, and now what? Almost a letdown. I've been running on a treadmill of disease and death. When it stops, I don't know what to do next. Get off or just stand there? I had been taking care of others for so long that it becomes who I am. And when I didn't need to do that anymore, the stop was so sudden I couldn't adjust. The out of town mourners left for home; the locals didn't know what to say to me anymore and came by when they had to. I was just as glad. I didn't know what to say to them, either. (Later, I very much wanted them to return. But I needed it to be in my time, and almost felt that I was entitled to it.) For a time I considered apologizing for putting them through so much.

Survival seems like a great idea, but in the immediate aftermath it appears somewhat overrated. Feelings come and go that it might have been quite pleasant not to be one of the few left standing. This is no longer survivor's guilt as much as it is survivor's envy. But I brush away these thoughts, knowing that I have my daughter Nicole still with me, along with Larry, her husband. And of course, my new grandson, Jamie.

I am now living in a four bedroom house alone. Sometimes wandering the halls, first to my bedroom, where Lenore died, then to Adam's room with the memories it evoked, finally to Stephanie's room. These are still their rooms in my mind, even though they rarely lived here. But stopping in and looking at them isn't depressing, simply sad. And this sadness somehow is comforting. I feel they are participating with me in the grief.

I need to learn to live alone, to be alone, even though I have been experiencing this, person by person as each died. Going for daily walks is good for exercise and for my mind. There is nothing like physical exertion to clear your head. At least for the moment.

By now I am feeling like a punching bag. I hardly had time to adjust to one disaster when the next one came down the road. When my son, Adam died I thought I was flattened. I felt I couldn't survive it and that if I did, I didn't want to. But time, as they say, is the great healer and as it went by, things got a little easier, just by its passage. Remembrances of using the *NOW* and how it saved me after Adam died glide in and then out of my mind. I try to hold onto them and for the few minutes they remain there is peace. But it is fleeting.

What made life difficult mostly, was processing thoughts about what I might have done differently to make or help Adam's life turn out better than it did. This would be followed by my peculiar sort of memory; I don't think of things as much as I watch them in my head. I would replay the events surrounding his suicide as vividly as if I were watching the whole thing on a video. Of course, the next move was to combine the two and beat up on myself with the idea that I should have done better, followed by images of finding him in the garage. I found no way of stopping these thoughts and I thought at times I would go crazy. There were times when I lived almost entirely in the past, processing these thoughts, but even then knowing that there never was anything I could have done differently. Logic didn't do a thing for me. I kept processing.

After Adam died, I discovered the *NOW*. It changed my life. You will remember that I compared it to learning to ride a bike. I thought I would never forget how to ride the bike nor will I forget how to use what I learned about *NOW*. Well, let me tell you, my arrogance came back and bit me. After Lenore and Stephanie die, all the grand plans I had for *NOW*, most of what I learned, go by the wayside. I am in a state of near collapse. It isn't just that I have forgotten how to use it, I can't even think. I have forgotten how to ride that bike. Or even that there is a bike to ride.

There were three different types of death in my family: cancer, heart disease and suicide. As I noted earlier, there are also three types of grief. Each type of grief needs to be treated as a stand-alone subject. One is the type that comes with the slow process of dying, such as Lenore and I experienced with her cancer. Lenore's death came with considerable warning and with it came anticipatory grieving. There were no surprises. Each day before she died, each part of each day, I grieved for the loss that was inevitably coming. This kind of grief requires a different resolution than one emanating from sudden death, because this one develops slowly. By the time death comes, the sponge has been squeezed fairly dry, so to speak. I had already allowed myself to grieve over a period of time. When the last moment comes for your loved one, with all its finality, grief is still going to happen. But the time factor may be shortened because you have already done so much grieving.

A second type of grief results from sudden death. This type of grief comes without warning and is sharp, sudden and can actually knock your breath out, leaving you unable to breathe for a short while. Grief like this arrives at your doorstep when you are having an ordinary, routine day. The unexpectedness of it and the lack of preparation can be devastating.

Although we always knew Stephanie had a weak heart and signals and symptoms were there for years, flashing a warning that something bad was coming, her death itself still came suddenly. The shock was as intense as if she had died without any warning, in spite of the symptom-messages that came to us over the years.

Adam's suicide led to a third type of grief. Initially, the experience was one of shock. As the grieving set in, it was made more complicated by the fact that his death was essentially violent and self-serving. I felt angry and hurt as well as bereft. Knowing that his death was voluntary only added to the crushing nature of the grief. It was only later that I could feel compassion for his action.

Having personally experienced all three types of grief, I can say with some certainty that none of them is easier than another; that no one is more difficult than another. Most likely, at the moment one of them hits you, that is the worst one of all, simply because it is present right then and there. But as time goes by, if you have experienced more than one, you will find that they are of equal magnitude.

NOW RETURNS

Because *NOW* has left and I am all alone, I have to restart my voyage of discovery. I know I'm not back at Square One but I don't know as yet what to do.

I feel there was something I could be doing with my mind to prevent these thoughts from dragging me down, but I can't find the magic answer. I read no books, I see no therapist, and I take no drugs to help me find peace. For no reason except inertia. A depression that I'm not aware of, perhaps. The sort of unconscious inertia that pulls you further under the waves without you feeling it.

Lenore's death came with considerable warning. And even though I knew what had happened to me after Adam, I was no better prepared to handle the mental strains. I have to reach into my soul to find what, with my unaddressed grief, is happening to me, what is about to happen to me, and most of all, what to do about it.

I need to answer my own questions. I start with the obvious: What is it that was dragging me down? The living in the past and future, of course. What I could do to get out of it was tougher. My first responses are the same: I can't get out of it; it is my nature and nothing I can do would help. This is a typical answer for someone who isn't thinking clearly. I think of hypnosis, of meditation, of therapy, of drugs, and wish I were into religion so I could turn there. I reject all of them and think, where can I go for solace?

After much searching it finally occurs to me that I didn't have to go anywhere. That there is no 'there' there. I needed to go within myself to find the answer.

I fail to find the answer at first, because it is too obvious and too close at hand. I look for something exotic and find something ordinary but elegant.

I am living in the past and suffering in the future. I need to get out of both. Where else could I go except the present? It is a true epiphany. I already taught myself, months previously, to live in what I have come to call the Holy *NOW*. But I was so overwhelmed that I have forgotten my own lessons.

I don't know what to do, but I do know that I can't go on the way I am. Something has to be cut loose or I will lose touch with reality. At least I know this and can do something about it before it is too late. Too late in the sense of becoming immobilized by feelings of depression, thus deepening the hole I find myself in.

You would think that after having already started to develop the idea of living in the *NOW*, I would be fully immunized to such feelings and that I would be fully prepared to deal with them once they cropped up. You would think, but you'd be wrong. It becomes ever clearer to me that the process of *NOW* has to be practiced every day, *especially* when things are going your way and your world is running smoothly. I thought I had been doing this but I also think I became distracted and wasn't watching. Obviously, I need to get back on track. A tidal wave of grief has come in.

After Lenore's death, I began a pattern of once more living in the past, examining the medical treatments she had received, and even thinking of the disagreements we had had and regretting that I couldn't have made her life a little better by never having them. I knew that her treatment was the best available because I was monitoring it. I had researched every known existing and soon-to-be existent treatment. I had examined the side-effects, rejecting some treatments out of hand based on these alone.

I then added a new twist to living in the past: living in the future. Worrying about how Stephanie would tolerate her mother's death; about Nicole not being able to show her new baby to her mother who obsessed on having grandchildren; and a number of other subjects, which were things that hadn't yet happened and might never happen.

I bounced back and forth from the past, which was over and done with, to the future, which might never happen. As much as I intellectualized this, I was unable to drive it from my head. I was convinced that there was nothing I could do about it except to accept it as a part of my life and therefore part of my way of thinking.

Less than three months later, in the midst of this turmoil, Stephanie died. More of the same for me. What could I or what should I have done differently for her medically? Did I miss something that might have saved her? Should I have brought her home that night? How was Nicole going to survive all this? How was I?

I can deal fairly well with thoughts of *one* of their deaths. But as soon as I do, thoughts of the other two come flooding in from the sides and I can't cope. I can handle one; I can't handle three. It becomes a matter of survival. I need to find a way out of my racing thoughts. I have lost my first tentative grip on the *NOW*. It is up to me to find my way back.

It finally comes to me that I need to learn to ride my bike again. Not starting from scratch, but just the same as riding a bike. You haven't done it for a while; you need to get back on and try again; but at bottom, you really didn't forget. You just need to make adjustments. And this is what I do.

It's a different bike now; and I need new tires. Dirt bike tires to dig into this new terrain. A stronger chain perhaps. But underneath it all there is the same me, and even though I have changed and adjusted to my new circumstances, I haven't really forgotten how to ride. The basics are still there.

I know where to go; I go within. The *NOW* is there waiting for me to bring it back. I have done it before and I can do it again. There is no choice if I am going to survive. This living, breathing idea that has served me so well in the past must be brought back in. I grasp the negative past that is enveloping me; it is almost tactile. I throw it overboard. Next, I take all the fearful future thinking that is coming at me and just drop it. As to the negative present, I simply ignore it.

Is all this easy? Absolutely not. The past wants back in. I say Stop! The fearful future is gnawing at the edges of my mind. I say Stop! And they stop. They know they aren't wanted here. I move on.

There is a certain strength that comes with knowing that even though the bombs of life are falling all around you, you aren't required to collapse. You can use this knowledge as power that gives you the ability to rise above the ashes.

Life is the sum total of our experiences. We relish the good, and learn from the bad.

RESURRECTION: RETURN FROM THE DEAD

The building blocks that I am using to reconstruct my life are once more laid before me. The tremendous struggle with the pain is receding and I need to reach within myself and allow some of the doors of the past to open. Positive doors that I allow to open at times of my choosing. I think, not of the bad times associated with Lenore's last years, but of the pleasant times from the entire 35 years. How can I do this? What will be the key to those positive doors? Photographs, of course. I go into our ancient photo albums and cannibalize the best representation.

I construct a collage, consisting of images going from Lenore's childhood, and coming full circle to some from the present time. Her friend Rosum is prominent in many of the later ones, as am I and Nicole, Adam, and Stephanie. These I mount on a board about 30 inches by 30 inches, and have the whole thing encased in a clear Lucite frame, which I hang from a wall in the front hall, facing the front door, so that it is the first thing you see coming into the house.

After Stephanie dies a few months later, I construct her own collage.

I remember that Hospice of the North Shore offers a counseling program for those who have suffered losses. I talk Lenore's friend Rosum into trying it despite her initial claims that she is not interested. I know how she is suffering, and she has no one to discuss it with. It seems appropriate to me, but she can't imagine telling her deepest feelings to a stranger. She goes, reluctantly, almost more to humor me than to seek emotional relief. Her grief counselor's name is Ellen, and Rosum immediately feels an attachment to her and possibly vice versa. The development of the relationship is wonderful. From not being able to tell someone the depth of her sadness, she evolves into a person who feels she can't live without Ellen.

Neither Nicole nor I feel we want such assistance. We feel we are strong enough without the need for grief counseling. But a few months later Nicole decides that she would like to have someone to talk to and a month or so later, I follow.

All three of us are going to grief counseling in the same time frame, but never together. Rosum goes the longest and when the terminal period of six months expires, she leaves with great reluctance. Nicole attends the shortest amount of time, because she feels it is time to move on. Each time I go, I feel I am wasting time because I have nothing to talk about. But eventually we find a lot to talk about and the sessions are very productive. They help me to experience the grief and allow me to feel the anger and sadness in a safe setting. I need to let the grief happen, especially since I have no choice, and then at the appropriate time, a number of months later, move on toward letting it go.

No longer taking control of Lenore's meds 24/7, I need instead to both let go of and take control of myself and how I choose to be in the world.

As we near the first anniversary of Lenore's death, Nicole and Rosum think it would be a great idea to honor her with a dinner at her favorite restaurant, Maggiano's. I think it is terrible idea. Too morbid and too weird. Like something from a bad movie. They convince me otherwise, saying that we need to have something on that date that is a celebration, not a funeral redux. This begins to make sense and I agree, realizing that it is a plan of healing for her survivors. The first anniversary dinner is anything but morbid. It is a celebration of her life. My trepidation is an unfounded invention of my mind. Eight of us sit down to dinner, including my toddler grandson, Jamie. Having him there is as it should be. He is the grandchild Lenore wanted and never saw. Her friend Rosum offers a toast to Lenore, saying that she is looking down right now, pleased with what she sees, approving the choice of restaurants. And particularly happy to see Jamie there, honoring her, as she blesses him. From that point onward, I realize that this will be an annual event that all of us will celebrate as if she invited us.

This plus lighting candles on the anniversaries of all their deaths and of their birthdays become living symbols of remembrance.

I start to rekindle some of my old interests. I resume my photography with my two friends, Lou and Barry. The three of us met in a nature photography club and were in the habit of going out each Saturday in various bird and landscape locations. But now that I am beginning to slowly reenter the world I once knew, I take a course in people photography and find a whole new direction. I stop shooting landscapes and animals and concentrate solely on homeless people in various parts of this country and of the world. It becomes my mission to make the invisible homeless population visible. I want the rest of us, particularly in more affluent areas, to see street people for what they are: fellow humans who never intended to be where they are now.

My grandson, Jamie, is soon a lively yearling. He is running around in the frenetic way of small children. I watch him and feel anxious. I'm afraid that he might pass out if he doesn't slow down, because of his bad heart. He is running in circles, starting from the living room, and then racing through the kitchen in a wide loop. The faster he runs, the more stressed I become. I am about to tell him he needs to stop and rest for a while, when it suddenly occurs to me that he *doesn't* have a bad heart, nor did he ever have one. It was Stephanie who did. And old memories come back. I remember watching her exerting herself and being torn: Should I tell her to stop to make me feel better or let her self-regulate and lead as close to a normal life as was possible under the circumstances? Usually I let her run if she wished; I didn't want my problem to become hers. And so, here I am, years later, transferring my anxieties from Stephanie to Jamie. Old fears die last. I calm myself down, smile, and enjoy Jamie's energy – in the *NOW*.

Even though I have gradually learned to let go of 'what ifs', some parts of fear of the future are still lurking in my shadows.

One of the most common areas in need of my new concept is an obsession with more loss. Each time I think I have it licked, I trip again. And one that really drives the point home is our dog, Chelsea. We have three dogs at the same time: a Yorkie, a Shih Tzu, and Chelsea, who is a mixture of Cocker and Poodle, and who was Nicole's originally. Chelsea developed diabetes and I give her a shot of insulin twice a day, every day. This requires me to gather the skin at the back of her neck and plunge the hypodermic needle in this spot. The diameter of the needle is very small and she apparently feels no pain. But in addition, I am getting very good at doing this, especially after having done it for Lenore, in her abdomen.

I get to the point that I no longer need to go to the vet to adjust the dosage; I can tell from Chelsea's actions that she needs an increase and I guesstimate what turns out to be the correct addition. But eventually, the insulin is no longer effective and she is losing control of her bladder and anus, in addition to walking into walls. She needs to be put to sleep. I don't have the nerve to take her to the vet myself but I have no choice and I can't ask Nicole. It isn't just the unpleasant nature of what I have to do. Mostly, it is one more loss and I don't want to deal with it.

The night before I am to take her in, Nicole's best friend, Heidi, phones and asks if I would like it if she does it for me. I don't hesitate to agree. That morning, it is raining fairly hard. Heidi arrives right on time. I hand her Chelsea and she drives off. I have an immeasurable reservoir of gratitude to Heidi for saving me in my hour of need.

Whenever I think of this event, it brings up old feelings of loss; feelings I can live without. Immediately, I have a need to reenter the *NOW*. And I do. I force myself to push back the memories of the past and deliberately bring my mind into the present and all the good it contains.

The crushing grief that has flattened me is now beginning to recede, however slowly. I am making a conscious decision that I no longer want, or need, to have it continue to control my life. I have chosen to regain it. The means, of course, is to return to the *NOW*. I have learned a valuable lesson. I thought that it had become part of me, but I hadn't practiced it enough. Every day. I now return to its warm embrace and the potentially destructive things that threatened to consume me for the past two years are in retreat. Although I have friends and extended family members at my side, it is my responsibility to right my own ship. I am the one with the problem and I know I have the tools to solve it. The tools are in *NOW*. I happily and gratefully take up the cudgel to fight back the misery and depression that threatens to engulf me. It would if it could but I won't let it. Once more I become a happy warrior. There is a dignifying and releasing feeling when you hold up your head again, take charge and accept responsibility for your own life and your own well being. Choose. Choose to rise again.

I realize that I am starting to develop a life of my own. I am becoming adept at broadening and deepening friendships. It was never a part of my nature in the past to seek these out, but now I have joined discussion groups on subjects that make one think, for instance about religion and politics. I have coffee with three friends each week to talk about anything that might come to mind, without an agenda.

One of these friends, in his 80s, asks me about my book and what I mean by Living in the *NOW*. He asks me to explain it. I tell him it would be easier if I have a specific example to chew on. Or I can simply make one up.

No, he says, I'll give you one: I don't enjoy getting older, along with its evil twins of tiredness and inability to do the things I once did. Frankly, I'm afraid of my health implications as each year goes by and I'm also afraid of dying badly. What can Living in the *NOW* do for me?

We are sitting in a coffee shop near his home, where two or three of us joined him every Thursday. I tell him that the *NOW* isn't some mysterious concept, but instead is quite ordinary. Right then, at that very moment, three of us are sitting in the coffee shop having a great time, just talking.

I remind him of his circle of friends, some of whom I also know, who all have a deep interest in his well-being. This circle, including me, represents an asset pool that he is able to call on whenever he needs to or wants to.

So, I ask, why does he have a need to live in the negative future? Contrast this, I tell him, with Living in the *NOW*, where he is already sitting and talking with two friends, in a golden moment, and with another small group of his friends ready and available for another coffee on another day. One simply needs to reach out and invite them.

Helping other people in this way is teaching me how to teach myself. Because I know how to, I have less need to take myself by the collar and pull me back into the *NOW*. Living there is becoming a part of me to the extent that I cannot imagine living outside it any more. One day, I am at one of my discussion groups all morning. I hear noon striking on a nearby church. Only then do I realize that I haven't thought, even once, about the past or the future. Do you see what is happening? I don't need to come back into the *NOW* because I haven't left it. It has so become a part of me that I've spent the entire morning being present. And the subject matter of the discussion hasn't been so intense that it is inherently distracting. I realize that the *NOW* has crowded out any possibility of negative space. My thoughts are so captured by the positive aspects that there just isn't enough room for negatives to enter.

I have been reaching out and involving myself in welcoming communities. In my case, it is by means of a spiritually-oriented church in a nearby town. I have become the semi-official photographer for special events. I start a monthly series of lectures on the general subject of poverty, which introduces my friends to something almost totally foreign to them; I enter mundane encounters as an opportunity for positive interactions. One means of reaching out is to make myself available to anyone who is experiencing grief.

I have a friend who lost a young child in a freak accident. She has been experiencing a crushing grief that I cannot really imagine. The minister of our church encourages me to tell her of the deaths of my two children, which I am reluctant to do, feeling that it might seem something like one-upmanship to her. He convinces me otherwise. She is grateful to hear from me. I do not try to tell her of living in the *NOW* simply because it is way too early in her grief. Instead I quote Bernie Siegel, and tell her not to say 'fine' or 'ok' if people ask how she is. I teach her how to respond with a number from 1 to 10, 10 being the best. As Bernie says, anything 6 or lower, and you get a hug. This is working for her. In the process of teaching her how to assess her grief on the 1-to-10 scale, I have learned how to apply this to Living in the *NOW*. Once you are able to determine the level of your own grief, you will be able to start on the road to the *NOW*. You need to understand the problem, and the depth of that problem, in order to bring back stability in your mind.

Because I am able to teach this, I learn. And almost every day, as I discover one more thing that is interfering with my peace of mind, I stop, listen to the chatter inside me, and think how this one particular circumstance exists only because I am not applying the *NOW*. At that exact point I throw off the yoke of the past, and the sister yoke of the future, and become centered in the present.

When I say 'almost every day', this is a fact. Thoughts come at me even in the most mundane aspects of daily living. And I have to keep practicing the *NOW* as if it were the first time; in many ways it is the first time. Each occurrence needs to be examined in a stand-alone way, and the *NOW* needs to be applied and utilized as if nothing had gone before it

It has come as a surprise realization that helping others is helping me, but only if that isn't my intention. The more I offer compassion to others, without any conscious hope of something beneficial to me, the more I gain personally.

I am learning to be able to tell people my story, not for sympathy, but to possibly help them in their time of grief. I begin to relearn to live in the *NOW* and to practice it every day. This is such a valuable resource for me that I want to share it, but only if someone wants me to; I don't want to preach. I find that the more I share it, and the more I help others, the more it helps me. The student has become the teacher, who then becomes the student once more.

The first years come to an end. I am still aware of the pain that is always ready to reenter my life. But now that I have become practiced in the daily usage of living in the *NOW*, I am forever conscious of the present and all the good it contains, instead of the weight of the past and the future.

The pain, although staggering, made me reach out to the lifeline of living in the *NOW* and not to keep the attachment to the past or the fear of the future.

Three people in my family died, but then three other family members entered my life: In addition to Nicole, my immediate family includes her husband, Larry, and their two children, Jamie and little sister Natalie, born three years after him. My two grandchildren have become an integral part of my living in the *NOW*. I discover that, without trying, I am virtually recording almost every action of theirs in my memory; they have been able to lay a bridge over the chasm of the lives they never knew. Although they never met Lenore, Adam or Stephanie, they have learned of them by means of their collages, and stories told to them by Nicole. Both Natalie and Jamie like to look at Nicole and Larry's wedding pictures. They refer to them as people they know well. Integration of loved ones into the present in this way is positive and affirming. It engenders warmth and security, rather than grief and fear.

I have become able to find myself by living in the *NOW*, which has opened me to the possibility of love. I already had it with Nicole and her family; with my new wife, Anne, entering my life, my circle is complete. Loving Anne doesn't that I've forgotten Lenore. Anne and I have both suffered the loss of a spouse. Paradoxically, for each of us, knowing that the other loved deeply in the past makes our present love deeper and our bond stronger. We have this thread, this common experience of having loved and then having our loved one die. This gives us a profound sense of connection.

Neither of us needed someone else to make our lives worth living. We were leading rich and full lives pursuing our interests, making contributions to the world, and enjoying our friends and family. We were ready to love and be loved because we were already happy living in the *NOW*.

I feel the time has come to acknowledge that the grief has been necessary, but that I also think the time has come to let go of some part of it.

I have been allowing myself to live in the *NOW* at various times in the past but it is time to crank it up full time. I can no longer afford the part-time experience; I have to have it with me always.

I have previously taught myself the value of *NOW* and how to accomplish it from time to time. But I know I need to become both the teacher and the student. The student needs the teacher once again, to learn how to live in the *NOW*, all day, every day. I carefully examine every event, large or small, to see how the *NOW* will apply. There are many failures. Many times I take two steps forward and one back. But eventually the extra steps forward pay off.

I feel the time has come to acknowledge that the grief has been necessary, but that I also think the time has come to let go of some part of it.

THE LAND OF *NOW*

A number of times over these years I have been asked how I was able to get through all this. How did I survive? At first I used to say it was *Creative Avoidance.* I couldn't think of one of my family member's deaths without all three crowding in. And so I avoided thinking about it, and I thought only about the present, not the past. But then I came to realize that what I needed to be doing was simply *living* in the *NOW*, pure and simple. The difference is that living in the *NOW* is an active *presence* rather than avoidance. You aren't running away from the past or the future. You are actively choosing to stay centered in the positive present. This is a learned process. I started living in the *NOW* then and have continued it in my daily existence, encouraging others to do the same.

Yes, the Buddhists say, *all life is suffering.*

It doesn't need to be.

I can, if I wish, relive those days of pain and grief, as if they were a month ago. Sometimes I see the events again and play them in my head as if they were a video tape. Living in the *NOW* allows me to just visit those times without being once more enveloped by them. But meanwhile, I continue to live my life, fully, in the everyday world of *NOW*.

What is the *NOW*? The *NOW* is the ability to live in the present and to be present in every living moment, which, of course, shifts as each minute goes by.

And what is the ability to live in the present? It is to recognize this minute for what it is and what it means to you. To recognize the magic and grandeur of the moment. Appreciating what is right here, whether sensory or mental. To gather up all the positives in your life right now and draw them into you.

To be present in every living moment is to be here, now. To be fully engaged in and focused on whatever you're doing or experiencing. Aware of what you're doing and who you're with, so that if you're sitting at a table talking to someone you're not thinking about what you did yesterday nor reading the titles of the books on the shelves around you nor planning tomorrow's activities.

The secret is not to dwell on what happened in the past and what might happen in the future, but to live in this very minute, to appreciate what is going on in your life right now. I look out the window of my office and I see blue sky and sunlight coming through a dense umbrella of leaves with birds singing and chipmunks calling to each other.

I am very lucky. Lucky to be alive and well and to have those who love me, near me. I have learned to look out the window and appreciate what is right in front of me without dwelling on what happened and what might happen. I feel a positive glow that some people see on my face. It comes from being so lucky and happy.

To be here, *NOW*, is really the secret of happiness and perhaps the secret of life. If only we can learn that lesson.

Taking control over what you are able to, and letting go of what you can't, is a key to Living in the *NOW*. This means becoming fully informed on the various facets that impact on your life, enabling you to make decisions about directions you want to take. You not only notice and appreciate the present as it comes to you, but you also shape it by engaging with it—getting involved in things that interest you, reaching out to other people, having new ideas.

Living in the *NOW* doesn't mean ignoring the world, and its events, past and future, around us. It means being in the world, recognizing things that have taken place in the past and are occurring in the present, and preparing for things in the future. The difference is that we are not obsessed nor immobilized by the past and future. And that we have made a conscious decision to leave past and future behind, until and unless we might choose to bring them along again temporarily. Having left them behind, we are now in charge of our own lives, instead of being at the mercy of our not-so-tender emotional reactions to the never-ending pain of grief.

Just be. Don't was. Don't will be.

THOUGHTS ON THE *NOW . . . PRIOR* TO GRIEF

I didn't fully come to the idea of living in the *NOW* until I was forced into it by grief. Yet when I look back on it, I can see that Lenore and I used some of these ideas during the course of her illness. And when we did, it was enormously helpful.

When Lenore was diagnosed with breast cancer and I with prostate cancer, our terrified moments came when we dwelt on fears of the unknown future. But when we were able to take ourselves in hand, realize that we were doing everything possible to make the best decisions that we could and get optimum care, then we could relax and enjoy the moment. We even enjoyed going for her radiation treatments together. Worrying about the future would not change it, it only took away from the pleasures ready for us to enjoy in the present.

When Lenore and I recognized that no treatment was going to cure her ovarian cancer, we chose to end the chemo and concentrate on enjoying what time we had left. This was liberating for us both. We didn't call it living in the *NOW*, but that's what it was. Whenever we started to think about our individual problems—right at that point—we brought ourselves back to the present. We practiced eliminating worries about the future. We refused to think of everything in the past that could have negative connotations. Instead we focused on what was happening right that moment and what steps were necessary to bring everything back under control. And it certainly paid off. I can't say, 'paid off in the end', because there is no end. It continues always.

If Lenore and I had been completely able to live in the present earlier in the process, a great deal of the fear of the unknown, the future, would have been lessened, and for that matter, unnecessary. Some of you, having read and thought about this book, may have the opportunity to practice living in the *NOW* before the next crisis in your lives. This is the really hard part. It's one thing to theorize and philosophize about the *NOW*, but when it comes to real life the difficulty sets in. Lenore and I were able to partly live in the *NOW*, but not completely. We were learning, teaching ourselves to live in the present, without having fully formed ideas.

Nevertheless, it is real life that benefits from the *NOW*, and the idea that this is a theory falls away, replaced by at least a semblance of peace of mind, because it is neither a philosophy nor a theory. It is reality itself.

As I said, you can only buy insurance *before* you need it, not *when* you need it. The *NOW* is almost in this category. Yes, you can learn it after you need it; but it is so much better for you if you learn it before you do, simply as a way of life. You can begin by practicing living in the *NOW* everyday. It will then be there for you through all of life's ups and downs.

Daily practice means exactly that: something that needs to be honed, much the same as learning a foreign language, *Use it or lose it*. You cannot hope to learn something this useful and valuable, to be used the rest of your life, if you do not have it completely embodied in your very being.

Let me give you an illustration of living in the *NOW*, *prior* to the grief of death. This is a real example in the life of someone I know.

My friend, Bill, had a recurrence of melanoma. The first occurrence was 12 years ago and was thought to have been beaten. Now it was back and more virulent than the first time. It became obvious that Bill was going to die. There was no cure. This was particularly sad because he had three children, the youngest just a few years old.

Then Bill learned of a new, experimental type of very aggressive chemotherapy. The problem was that it was largely untested and the investigators of the drug were looking for someone just like Bill, in order to continue their trials. Bill was tremendously tempted. He discussed it with his wife and told her that the upside was he might have an additional 6-12 months to spend with her and their children; the downside was that the side effects almost certainly included being virtually incapacitated as well as massive vomiting and general weakness. They had a terrible decision to make, not uncommon for people in a similar situation. To live a few months longer but under dire circumstances, or to accept a shorter life that would include more quality time with his wife and children.

He – they – chose the latter. To live in the present moment instead of trading quality for time. It was a variation of living in the *NOW*. They taught themselves to live every precious minute of the time they had together. In many ways, the relatively brief time they had with each other was to be envied, not pitied. When Bill died, his family felt they had truly lived as a unit, perhaps more than they did prior to his illness.

❖

As I neared the completion of this book, I tried to put myself in the place of the reader. I succeeded so well that I felt if I were in need of help with my grief, I might find all this interesting, but wouldn't know where to start. How could I begin living in the very *NOW* that I would need to do. That I would want to do.

But I wouldn't know where to begin. Sure, I'd say, Jack was able to bring back his sanity and to resume living a 'normal' life again. But how would I apply that to me? I have no idea what the first step would be.

I thought about this and couldn't even answer my own question. I didn't know how I'd tell someone how to apply this directly to her own life, his own grief. And so I did the only thing possible. I thought out the very first step that I, or anyone else, would take; would have to take. The first step is to accept your grief as your reality. This is simply something that has taken over your life. Don't walk away from it; you couldn't if you wanted to. Instead, walk *into* your grief. Allow it to become part of you without resisting. Allow it to become part of you. That's how the first Step begins. Then there are other steps to take. But I'm getting ahead of myself.

I created Ten steps to surviving your grief. Turn the page, start them, and let the healing begin. This book will do for you what it does for me. If you let it.

TEN STEPS

TEN STEPS FOR SURVIVING CRUSHING GRIEF BY LIVING IN THE *NOW*

These are paths for you to take to guide yourself back from your world of grief, into a new world of healing that is waiting for you to enter. The First Step is the logical one for all of us to take. But the rest of them, the other nine, aren't meant to be strictly linear. Perhaps you will find yourself doing two Steps at once, or skipping a Step for awhile, or even turning back to a Step previously passed by. That is all to be expected. It also is to be expected that you'll find yourself coming back to some Steps over and over again. In some ways the Steps are like a spiral staircase. Or think of the intertwining strands of the double helix of a DNA. You move forward, then find yourself dealing with an issue you thought you'd finished. Except that you realize you are approaching it from a different vantage point than you had before. And you cross over to the other strand and return to a previous Step. You come to a new understanding and a more fruitful way of doing that Step.

As I mentioned in the Introduction, don't feel that you need to follow these Steps in order. You need to start with Step #1 but after that your own state of mind might dictate that you should go, for instance, from Step #6 back to Step #2 and then forward again to Step #5. The choice and the decision is yours to make.

STEP 1. LET GRIEF HAPPEN.

Unlike fog, grief doesn't arrive on little cat feet; instead, it arrives in towering waves that engulf and own you, all at once. Learn to *ride* the wave when it comes, because like all waves, it will come and it will go, and is not a constant state. Even at this early stage, it comes, washes over you, then subsides for a while.

Someone has died, or you have experienced some other devastating loss, and grief has virtually taken over your life. Don't even try to resist the grief; let it happen. There isn't any point in resisting it. It will take place no matter what you do.

In my case, after three people in my immediate family died, I went to a grief counselor because I *wasn't* grieving. At least not enough. I felt it was very unhealthy, mentally, to resist this grieving process. The problem was, I wasn't aware of resisting it. It just *was*.

I found that I wasn't able to grieve for only one of my family members at a time. When I tried to do so, memories of the other two came flooding in. I might have been able to handle one, but not three. As a result, I pushed all grieving out of my head, even though it was unconscious and involuntary.

Obviously, this is not a good thing. The best thing to do is to let the grieving process come about. Allow waves of grief to *happen*. What this consists of can very well be related to cultural customs. Someone British, for example, might be tightly controlled, while a Mediterranean person might be inclined to be much more emotional. Both are doing what they need to do and would be very uncomfortable in role reversals.

One of the first aspects of grief is often anger. Yes, anger. You might be angry because you feel the doctor could have done better. You might even become angry at your loved one for dying and leaving you behind. You might be angry at God. Thoughts like these aren't illogical or unreasonable or unnatural. Your mind is as tight as a knot. Sometimes you feel like striking out. The problem is, there's no one, and no thing, to strike out against.

There are other feelings also, of course. And sometimes these can be stronger than anger. They can be manifested by pangs that are so intense they are almost physical in their sensation of pain. I am thinking of the moment I learned that my daughter Stephanie had died. My mind absorbed this as if it were physical pain. I felt exactly as if I had just walked into a very real brick wall. Sadness enveloped me as surely as if I were being pulled under water.

One other feature that gave me a great deal of difficulty was the feeling that I was unable to cope. It was too much for me; I felt ground down. I couldn't cope because I no longer wanted to cope. And I no longer wanted to because I thought I had lost the ability and didn't want to fight a losing battle. But I realized I had no choice except to keep going.

Other aspects of grief that I experienced myself were strong feelings of emptiness and longing for Lenore, Adam and Stephanie. It is too easy to say that the emptiness and longing are contained in the mind and not in the physical world; but the emptiness is virtually tangible. Something you can almost reach within yourself and touch.

You will find that reading these words will give you permission to feel many different things.

Think of grief as a good, and a necessary, process in your life. When someone who was a vital part of your life has died, or you had some other devastating loss, it would be unrealistic to believe that you could simply wish away the pain by reciting feel-good mantras. You need to experience the grief from your head to your toes and into your emotional soul. In order for you to finally purge the anguish from your mind, you need to confront and then accept it. It goes with the territory of living. You will have arrived in living in the *NOW* of grief. Living in the *NOW* does not necessarily mean being pain-free; instead it means that you have started the journey.

You will know that the pain isn't going to go away. But things will start to get easier, one small step at a time. This will help:

- Pain will come in waves, but there will be spaces between the waves, spaces that will allow you to catch your breath. Sometimes there are big waves; sometimes small. Sometimes they seem high enough to overwhelm you. But the height will gradually come down and the spaces between will lengthen. Time itself will become your friend and healer.

- Seek out others for connections and comfort. Let people rally around you. You are going to find that they might stay away because they simply don't know what to say. Let them know that their presence is meaningful to you.

- Set priorities. Focus your available energy on those things that are most essential to you, such as enjoying your loved ones or managing your expenses and your money. If managing your money is a major burden for you, or something you don't do well, get help from someone else and do the things you *can* do.

- Give yourself permission to have moments of happiness. Enjoy beautiful music, cheer at the touchdown, pet the dog. It's ok to have these moments of serenity in the midst of grief. And it's all right when you discover they don't last.

- Most of all, forgive yourself for sometimes being swamped by these waves. You can definitely survive them and you will probably ride the next wave successfully.

Only then, when you have allowed the grief to happen, and are not suppressing it, will you be able to move on to the next step.

STEP 2. TIME TO MOVE ON

Eventually, you will come to the conclusion that you have suffered enough from grief and it's time for you to move on with your life. What does 'eventually' mean? Good question, for which only you have the answer.

Recognize that your grief has gone on for six months, twelve months, or whatever time period feels right to you, and you'll realize that it's time to lessen the hurting as much as you can, and to move on. You'll know when it's the right time when you're there.

But how will you know? The first signal is that there will be longer periods of time between waves, and the waves themselves will not be as intense as before. You will have more breathing room; more time to try to regain your footing.

The fortunate thing about Living in the *NOW* is that you don't need to announce it to anyone. For that matter, no one knows you've moved there. But they might notice that some of the weight has been lifted from you and from your face.

It isn't time to stop hurting — this will remain for a while — but it is time to stop making the hurt the central piece of your life. It is a thread in the tapestry of your life, but understand clearly that it isn't the *whole tapestry*.

That thread is always going to be there in your life. But you are starting to find that you can deal with this thread of pain when it makes its presence felt. And you are ever more aware of all the other vibrant threads in your tapestry. The many joyful, meaningful moments you have. In fact, you realize that the thread of pain can be a source of strength and connection to others.

The time has come for you to start taking care of you; to start the process of being good to yourself. A friend, who lost a young child, told me that she is learning to take care of herself. This consists of doing things in daily life that she wants to do. Others might think she should be doing otherwise, but she disregards them. More importantly, she has learned to say no. If she feels that there is something she doesn't want to do, she chooses not to do it. If friends and family have a hard time with this, she simply feels they have a problem; she herself doesn't.

Sometimes misfortune and illness lead us to the light as much as into the dark.

When we think about a loved one who has died, we regard our sense of loss as coming from this love. Correctly. And we feel that the love is a physical thing because we remember the attachment we had for the person physically present, whom we could touch. But physicality is only a part of love. Love isn't dependent on physical presence; mostly it comes from our inner core, our emotional being. Yes, your loved one has left you, but only the physicality has left you. The inner structure of the love you had isn't past tense. It is in the present. It will not leave you. Your grief will eventually lessen, but your love need not. It will endure and will sustain you in the coming years.

Until now, this pain, this grief, has been the lens through which you have viewed absolutely everything. Now your mission becomes making your present day, your present life, the new lens. Continued grief, with no end in sight, could have a deleterious effect on you. It can have a similar effect on those around you, whether relatives or friends. They will start to feel that it is difficult to have a normal conversation with you, not wanting to go near 'that subject'.

Your new lens is the lens of clarity. You will see the positive things in your life that you haven't been able to see until now and you will learn to focus on them.

Reinforcements:

Right about now I can imagine that you are wishing you had an exercise or two to reinforce what you've just read. Anticipating this, I have a few for you.

- Sometimes you will experience waves of grief or by negative thoughts from your loss at times when you really need to be doing something else, such as finishing your grocery shopping. Here's what you do as your exercise: tell yourself that although you need to grieve, you don't need to grieve in the grocery store. And so you make an appointment with yourself. You choose to set aside time later today when it is much more convenient, or even tomorrow, such as 2:00 in the afternoon, when you have nothing else on. You write it in your calendar. Make an appointment with yourself that is no different than any other appointment you make. Then, at the appointed hour, you sit down in a quiet private place and you take time to grieve.

- One of your friends or relatives tells you there is something you 'should' be doing. You don't feel it's right for you. So don't do it. Tell yourself, 'No, I'm not going to do that. I'm going to do what I feel is right'. Do what you want to do. Gauge what is right for you for that day.

- Try out having short conversations with others about things other than your grief–topics that used to interest you or that you think might interest them. This will, for brief moments, change the lens through which you're looking at the world. Don't try to do this for sustained periods if you aren't ready. Just for a few minutes.

STEP 3. START TO COPE WITH BEING ALONE. *NOW.*

I can imagine many of you saying, 'Suddenly? My husband was dying over a 20 month period. What's sudden about that?'

This is why it's sudden: the day after a loved one dies, even after a long illness, you feel like your life just fell off a high cliff. You have nothing more to do. No one to care for any more. The suddenness, the emptiness, catches you by surprise. You thought you would be prepared for this day, but you can't prepare. From that day forward we are all suddenly alone.

You look across the dinner table at the space that was filled for so long and has now been empty for so long. You get in the car into the previously unaccustomed driver's seat. You wake up in the morning, and as the haze of sleep leaves, you once more realize you are alone in your bed. These are not some sort of epiphanies that just popped into your head; they are near-daily intrusions on this phase of your life. You are trying, with some silent desperation, to achieve what passes for normalcy. Still needing to adjust.

There is no state of denial here. You are quite aware that the chair across from you has been empty for some time; you know you are now the driver, not the passenger; and your bed has become larger than you ever wanted it to be for want of another being.

You have entered a winter of your life. A world you never made and never asked for, but you are here nevertheless. Three words come to mind: alone; aloneness; and loneliness. Ohmigod! you say to yourself. What am I doing here? Where are all my friends? Who took my life away?

You probably know someone who has been described as a loner. Other than in a few cowboy movies, this isn't considered a compliment. Most of us want people.

Your loved one has left and you're still here. You are still standing but you sure don't feel like it. You feel like crumbling. Even though I didn't, crumbling sounded like a wonderful idea to me.

You are alone in many ways even if your family and friends are right at your side. These others suddenly feel like *The Others*. They can't possibly know or feel what you feel. Alone is a physical fact, but aloneness is an attitude. It's pure misery that derives from being alone. Loneliness is a first-cousin to aloneness. After you have tried out both of them and learned that you hate them both, come to *NOW*. Come back to the Ten Steps. I say, 'come back', because the present – neither the past nor the future – is where you belong. It is your true nature and you need to return to it as soon as possible.

You have no need to be caught in the aloneness of your grief; you have no need to be stuck in the loneliness. Your life is already filled with people who are waiting to be there for you.

This is your time to reach out and let them.

Paraphrasing A.E. Housman: Alone and afraid/In a world I never made.

Of course you're suddenly in a world you never made. But you don't have to be alone. And you don't have to be afraid.

You can hope that your friends and family will be there to support you now and in the coming years. You can hope, but don't expect it to happen. Unless you do something to make it happen. Be present in *their* lives. Don't expect that their support will last past the first few months unless you take action to insure it. Here's what you do: remain a vital part of their lives exactly the same as before your loss occurred. Go to their weddings, attend their graduations. Even though you are now alone, don't make it seem so. Act as if your missing person were right with you. You will become a fifth wheel only if you allow it.

A few months after the loss you might notice that the invitations and phone calls have dried up. This is only natural. They don't know what to say to you. They don't know which subjects are off limits and simply too sensitive. This is when you take the initiative and call them. Say that you notice they don't call any more and that you realize they don't know what to say. Tell them you wouldn't know either if you were in their shoes. But by telling them there are no sensitive subjects you will be giving them permission to say anything. Make it easy for them. You will be admitted once more to normal society.

Let me illustrate by telling you the story of Claudia:

She and her husband had a great life and a marvelous future in front of them. He was building his career, and he and Claudia were building their lives in many directions at once. They had two teenagers, a boy and a girl, to whom they were deeply devoted. They had strong connections with a handful of friends with whom they socialized and interacted; most had children also but one couple didn't.

With no prior symptoms, Claudia's husband died suddenly at 45. Now she was left with two teenage children, taking on responsibilities and having to make decisions she neither counted on nor wanted. No choice, however.

As much as she was in a state of shock, so were her friends. After the initial mourning surrounding the funeral they wanted to reach out to her but didn't want to intrude on her grief. They didn't know what to say. They didn't know what the right thing to do was. And so they did nothing and essentially stayed away. At first, Claudia just accepted this; she didn't know what to say either and didn't want company. She started to withdraw within herself.

But after a while, Claudia's loneliness became unbearable. She was already in grief and missing the daily interaction with her husband, but now she started feeling the pain of having no friends to connect with. She didn't like being without adult company, but she didn't know what to do. She wondered if her friends didn't want to be around her anymore. But then she realized that this was new territory for all of them. They almost felt like awkward strangers, she and they. Maybe they weren't deserting her; perhaps they were just uncomfortable. She wanted to pick up the phone, call one of her friends and offer to go out for coffee. Just like in the past. But how could she do that? Shouldn't she wait until they called her? No. This could go on forever. As difficult as it seemed, she needed to be proactive; it wasn't part of her nature but this was no time to even think about that.

Her first call was to her best friend Francie. 'Gee', she said, 'I haven't heard from you and Bill for a long time.'

'Oh, Claudia, I'm so happy to hear from you. I didn't have the nerve to call. I just didn't know what to say.'

'Neither did I, Francie, but now I do know what to say: let's go out for coffee! When are you free?'

Do you see what happened? Claudia was beginning to return to the present. She might never have heard it expressed as living in the *NOW*, but she realized it was time to start to cut the cords that tied her to the negative past. She was still respecting the memory of her beloved husband, but it became time to move on and not have her grief remain the central thread of her life. It would become a significant thread of the tapestry of her life but it would no longer be everything. She had two children who were also grieving. They had already lost their father. Claudia determined that it was now time for their mother to return.

In effect, Claudia needed to reinvent her life. To rediscover the things that were most meaningful in it. The daily newspaper gave her a clue. She noticed which subjects she turned to first, those of her greatest interest. In her case it was politics and baseball. She was lucky there was no shortage of either to read about or actually do. Next, she called Alice, a baseball nut. Very soon the two of them were at a Tuesday afternoon game. Her kids were pleasantly surprised by this turn of events. Their mother was finally opening her door and letting others in. She was also giving permission to her children to do the same.

Look at what else happened: Francie and Alice wanted to support Claudia but didn't know how. They couldn't bring themselves to reach out. And so Claudia reached out; she was supporting them! New dimensions entered their lives. Francie got her best friend back and Alice got a baseball friend. Claudia had gone to games before with her husband but never with a girlfriend. It had never occurred to her.

A whole new world opened to all three of them.

Reinforcements:

- Call a friend or family member and plan to get together. Make the focus one of mutual interest rather than just your grief.
- Do the same with a friend or family member you are afraid you're losing touch with.

STEP 4. EXAMINE THE PAST

The past, after all, is where the grief resides. ('Past' is a relative term. It might mean six months ago or a few years ago.) Examine it by asking yourself if you've really had enough pain, or do you need to stay where you are for a while longer?

Remember, however, it is the grief itself you want to lessen. You don't need to ignore the events that caused the grief. *You are certainly not trying to forget your loved one.* You will then empower yourself to revisit those tough memories whenever you wish, for whatever reason, good or bad. And then leave them once again.

When you are visiting the past, you don't have to limit yourself only to reminders of bad things that happened to you. There were probably positive times that were mixed in. Here's an example: when my wife, Lenore, was in the final months of her life she had the air conditioning in the bedroom near arctic levels. With a heavy comforter up to her neck, the only part of her that remained visible was her near-bald head. Our small dog, a Shih-Tzu, loved her and would jump up on the bed and lick the top of her head. Lenore would scream laughing and try to hide under the covers. What happened? We managed to bring a little levity into tough circumstances. I now can happily revisit those times that were interspersed with the difficult ones. I can also revisit good times that are standalone. That have no relation to anything bad. For example, Nicole and Larry's wedding. Stephanie, of course, loved every minute of it as did Lenore. To this day, it is a marvelous memory, as I picture the two of them, their eyes shining, and glorying in the moment. This was a joyous occasion with nothing but positives.

These positives are as much a part of our narrative as the negatives and it would be a mistake to focus only on the latter. This is the true meaning of Examine The Past. Yes, examine it, but don't ignore the positives just as you won't think only of the negatives. You will become the one in control and *you* will choose when you revisit and you will decide which side of the equation you will allow in the door.

In the beginning, grief is in control. Let it be. This is as it should be. Eventually, your goal needs to be that you will control the grief. You will let it come in when you invite it, and you will tell it to stay out when it is not invited. You are the only one who may to do the inviting. At this point you will begin to realize that control is returning to you.

There is one conclusion that is inevitable, and it is this: Grief and pain are in the past part of your life. Sooner or later you need to leave the past and live only in the present except for brief visits. But before you do this, you need to understand that your pain has become a part of you and is not going to leave willingly. Like an in-law who came to help out for a while and then stayed on, seemingly forever because no one asked him to leave. But now a thank you and goodbye are required. He will understand, and the parting will be gradual but agreeable. A thread of pain will always remain as a piece of the tapestry of your life, but you won't let it be the dominant pattern.

Reinforcements:

- Choose which aspects of the past you want to remember and cherish. Then experiment to find your way of holding them, a way that fits your style and strengths. Save mementos, jot down memories or dictate them into a tape recorder, paint pictures—whatever works for you. When you're ready, give away or throw out items which you don't feel you need to keep, especially if they cause you pain. In my case I made large collages of photos after each family member died and had them mounted behind clear Lucite. I hung them up for a few years and then didn't need to any more. I keep them stored away in a place where I can look at them any time I choose to.

- Practice mentally dropping in and out of the past. Set aside a moment or moments in the day when you will deliberately remember some of the good things about the past. Then equally deliberately, return your focus to the present.

- Consider establishing some rituals to remember your loved ones. These can range from lighting a candle on the anniversary of their deaths and birthdays, to having a special dinner of remembrance on the anniversary of their deaths, to saying *good night* to their pictures each night. The goal is to have these remembrances be meaningful but also be controlled and limited.

STEP 5. EXAMINE THE FUTURE

The future doesn't contain grief; one of the things it can contain is fear. Fear, for example, that something bad is going to happen in the future. And this fear needs to be addressed and sent away. It doesn't live here anymore.

Fear, perhaps, that another death might happen. Certainly another might, but more than likely, one will not. This is one of those aspects of life over which we have absolutely no control. But we don't need to control everything. Instead we turn our backs on the fear and walk away from it.

Fear that you can't handle your life and you might go to pieces. Of course you are able to handle your life. You have thus far and you will continue to do so. You will not go to pieces. The loss that has caused your grief was seemingly overwhelming and more than you could cope with. But you have already learned that this is not true. Your family, your friends, and you yourself have rallied round you. Life is hard but you know you can and will survive.

Fear that nothing good will ever happen to you again. Why not? You have suffered a severe loss, but nothing in that loss will prevent good things happening to you once again. This fear can easily be self-fulfilling. If you let it. One day you will cross the border and allow your life to resume. Not as it was before, because it won't. But it will resume as a new life and good things will come into it because at the right time you will allow them to.

Fear of disease or poverty. Any one of us might have money problems in the near future. Many people are a testament to this. Just as easily, some dreadful disease might overtake us. But very likely, ten years from now, we will still find a way to pay our bills and be able to manage any medical condition we may have. It would be foolish to spend the good years of our lives worrying about potential bad things in the future. Right now is all there really is. Not everything in life needs to go smoothly in order for us to maintain the happiness that is our core.

The problem is that none of these fears is totally unrealistic. They could happen. But we could just as well fear getting hit by a car and stay home all day. The problem is more accidents happen at home than on the street.

Our focus on the future draws us away from fully living in the present moment. We are so worried about what *might* happen that we don't engage in what *is* happening now. We lose sight of what we have.

Our minds tend to exaggerate the possibility of something going wrong and underestimate the probability that things will be OK. And we also underestimate our ability to cope with the problems or losses that we may encounter. We are more resilient than our fears lead us to believe.

We can plan prudently for things that reasonably might happen by buying insurance, writing a Living Will, repairing frayed relationships where possible, and so forth. And then we can let go and refocus our attention on the *NOW*.

My personal fear of the future is that another of my loved ones will die. A wave of fear approaches and I begin to think about what *might* happen. Again. This comes at me frequently. But it doesn't stay because I choose not to let it stay. I immediately latch onto the *NOW* and allow myself to realize how good things are. Right now. As long as I stay centered on this path, my fears have no place on it. The wave recedes.

But, you know, you or one of your loved ones doesn't have to die for you to need the *NOW*. It can be something a lot less permanent but harder to cope with because it's chronic. Let me give you an example from my own life. Recently, I thought that it would be a good idea if I bought insurance for long-term health care, in case I ever had to go into a nursing home for months or years. Even though I am in perfect health at the moment things can change, as we all know.

So I checked it out and read all the brochures. Then my mind started to project. If I got to be about 92 years old and then became incapable of taking care of myself, I might have to move into an assisted living facility. This would effectively compress my life from potentially the whole world into just one room, or at the most, one building. It would be something like being confined to a comfortable prison. This was quite a depressing thought. Then I thought it through. I'm not 92 or even close to it. At some future date I might have to live in this confined way. But I don't now and why should I choose to live a thousand emotional deaths thinking about something in the future? Actually, this conclusion applies to a future negative event next week as much as it does to me at 92. There is no need to put yourself in the mental wringer of what could happen one day. Even if you knew it *would* happen one day, that day isn't now, is it? Today is as bright as you choose to make it. Realizing that today might be a cloudy day doesn't make it a bad day. It just makes it a cloudy day. But back to the assisted living idea. Two things: you're not in such a facility at the moment, so why trade the good things going on in your life right now for something negative down the road? Second, suppose you are in one of these facilities. It doesn't have to be as bleak as I painted it. If you visit one you might find a bunch of the residents sitting in the lobby. Some are quite happy; some are neutral on the subject of contentment; and others look borderline miserable. All in about the same proportions of ordinary people as you would see on a downtown street at noon. Your temperament will follow you.

Living in fear neither stops bad things from happening nor enables you to be better able to cope with them if they come.

Just as it is time to leave the past, it is time to leave the feared future. You have no need for past pain nor future fears. It is time to live in the present. The future isn't only fear; it might contain hope. The reemergence of hope signals that you are ready to move forward, from the future to the present.

While it's not as crippling as living in the feared future, living in the wistful future also keeps us from savoring what we have now. Since none of us is going to live forever, we all have to face the fact that some future events will go on without us. Another example from my own life: I was looking at my six year old granddaughter and thinking how she might look in about 20 years. I wondered if I would be around in 20 years to see her get married. The inference is that I might not be, and this would make me sad.

But why would I choose to do that? She is here now and very much in my life. I am able to look at her every day and watch her grow – in height and in learning about life. And so what did I do?

I immediately dropped the thoughts of 20 years from now and enjoyed the present. There she was in front of me in all her 6 year old glory. What a foolish trade it would have been to live in the wistful future and not be able to enjoy the fabulous *NOW*.

A variant of fear of the future is when we're anticipating changes that will affect us. We often dread what we think we might lose, don't see what we might gain, and inflict pain on ourselves in the present by dwelling on our negative imaginings. Let me illustrate by a scenario:

It is early June. Your daughter has just graduated from high school. At the end of the summer she will be going off to college, a thousand miles away.

You have two children. Your son is already in college. Now that your daughter has graduated, you are quite aware that you will soon be alone in a house that once held three people.

This is a loss. No one has died, but a loss nevertheless. You are grieving now in anticipation for your loss that will absolutely come in the fall. And who can you tell of your grief? Not your daughter nor your son. It is very hard for you to remove it from your mind. No one has died, but you will be left to yourself as if someone had died. Making matters worse, your friends are congratulating you on your success as a parent. Don't they understand that you are suffering? Can't they see past the surface facts? Apparently not.

You think of all the wonderful times the three of you had while they were growing up. Good times that will never come again. And you realize that when they go off to college, they will never come home again. They will get jobs out of college and, being used to independence, will get an apartment some- where so they can be their own persons. They will no longer be your children, dependent on you for everything, but instead you will all be peers. It's going to be miserable.

As you think about this you will realize you have com- pletely considered both the past and the future. Not the unhappy past but quite the opposite. The very happy past is making you realize what you will be missing. And the future holds nothing for you without your children.

It isn't only the negative past that can drag you down. As we have just seen, the wonderful past can do the same. And the awful future that is staring you in the face is not to be ignored. *Or so you think.*

Until . . . .

Until you remember the *NOW.*

You decide to pull yourself together and reenter the pres- ent. You appreciate all the great things going on in your life that have nothing to do with your children. Perhaps you are an active member in your garden club and are valued by your fellow members. You have marvelous friends who have invari- ably supported you thru past life changes. You have an entire wonderful life completely apart from your children. So why, I ask, do you want to focus on negatives, when you can choose not to? For that matter, why do you choose to look at the life changes of your children as negatives? They are doing what they should be doing. Would you prefer that they not go to college and instead sit home with you, being resentful for the life they could have had? A life they did not have because of feelings of guilt they felt from you.

Of course not.

It is at this juncture that you can appreciate the perfect opportunity to practice the *NOW*. And to practice it every day. You allow yourself to remember the wonderful times the three of you had together as they were growing up. But you are able to relate these thoughts to living the life you are enjoying in the present and that you have been living in the present for some time. You will be able to see your children for who they are. They are the result of what you have created from your life and brought to their lives. You recognize that you get great pleasure relating to your son as an interesting young adult and realize that you'll enjoy this next stage in your relationship with your daughter, too. They are already successful, thanks to you, for what they have learned from you all these years. And you are a success for having done so.

Each day now you remember and appreciate the wonderful past and you realize the equally wonderful future that lies ahead for all three of you. But mostly you focus on the present, the *NOW*, that is already here. You are able to practice living in the present all day every day. And you do exactly that: you practice it. Not just once a day, but throughout the day at every opportunity. And you will come to realize that you have nurtured this ability simply because you have taught yourself to live it. To live what you have chosen for yourself: the ability to choose to drop the negative past and feared future and open the door to your positive past and future, but mostly to fix your sights on the present and all it holds.

Your children are both in college; they are fruitfully launched on the life you have provided for them; and by observing you and the terrific things the *NOW* is doing for you, they start living in the present themselves. You have brought joy to them and they have brought joy to you. And it has no end.

I'm thinking of another such situation from my life. I have a friend who is in a prominent position in a large organization. He is in charge of about 150 very talented people. He's good at what he does, loves it, and is highly respected by his peers, employees and upper management. The problem is that nearing 70 he is being eased out, not of the organization, but of his position.

Similarly, no one has died but he is already in grief. His life is coming to an end. Not his physical life but the life that has such deep meaning for him. In his mind the title, the respect, and the perks will all end and as they do he will have nothing to replace them. Life as he knows it will be over.

What to do? He can't see anything but gloom. But as tough as it seems his world simply hasn't come to an end. He's living in a destructive future. He can't see beyond that mind set. He must . . . yes, must . . . *rip* himself out of this tomb that is enveloping him. I say *he must* because I can't do it for him.

It is time for him to stop what he is doing and to live in the *NOW*. He needs to think of all the good things in his life that are there now which he has bypassed in his thinking. He can still remain doing the work he has always done; but he will not be in charge. He can look at the family that loves him and bring his mind back to a reunion with them. It is not too late for him to realize that there is a world outside his profession. He can learn new things, new paths. But first he needs to free himself of the negative future and to teach himself to live only in the present. The *NOW*.

Reinforcement:

Write your fears or worries on index cards. Put a worry on one side of a card. On the other side put:

A. Why this fear/worry is exaggerated or unrealistic

B. What you can reasonably do about it

C. How you can let it go and refocus on the *NOW*

For example, my friend who is fearful of being forced into a job change due to his age could write this worry on one side of a card:

'My life will be over when I lose my position at age 70'.

On the other side of the card he could write, for example:
A. I will still have important responsibilities in my job. My job isn't my whole life.
B. Analyze my new position and find a way to tailor it to my interests. Expand my activities outside of work.
C. Be mindful of the good things going on in my life right now. Appreciate my family, enjoy my interests, and do things outside of work which are fulfilling.

For example, my friend in his 80s, whom I mentioned earlier might write 'dying badly' on one side of one card. On the other, he could write:
A. Remember a past hospital experience when I was not alone
B. Follow medical advice, write a Living Will, maintain friendships.
C. Focus on the pleasure I'm feeling now in having coffee with friends, reading a book, listening to music.

Keep your cards in a place where you can refer to them if the fear or worry comes again.

STEP 6. EXAMINE THE PRESENT.

The present, obviously, is our target, our goal.

Even if you're disabled or out of money, there are good things going on in your life in spite of these misfortunes. Since you're not yet dead, what is going on in your life that's pleasant or meaningful? If your first instinct is to say, 'Nothing', look closer. There are things in your life that *could* be meaningful or pleasant but are easily brushed aside while we choose to focus on the pain. Think about your family, your friends and things you like to do and do well. These might have been pushed into the background while you were grieving, but now it's time to resurrect them. Your friends and family are in that background waiting for you to let them know it's all right to come on in. Let them know the door is open again and that you are welcoming them.

Making connections and reconnections with others will be tremendously rewarding for you and them. Often, you will find that old relationships will change. Some will weaken; some, on the other hand, will strengthen. See those changes as natural and accept them for what they are. Start being open to new friendships.

Having given up the past and the future as sources of pain and fear, it is time to learn to live in the *NOW*. The present is sitting here, just waiting for you to show up. You need to recognize and join it, so that it becomes you and you become it.

What is the meaning of life? People ask that question, realizing that there is no answer. But I have one:

It is not in a future heaven.

It is not in our past accomplishments.

The meaning of life — as it virtually says in the Bible — is here and in the *NOW*.

But what if the *NOW* is awful? A legitimate question. Why would you want to live in the *NOW* if you can't stand the *NOW*? Then what do you do? One of two things. First, examine your life at the present. Are there good things going on in it, as there are with me? A great family and strong home base plus Anne, the new love in my life. With this examination you might discover that there are a lot more positive things going on than you think.

I found small blessings almost every day, even when life was at its most difficult. They came in moments of connection with Lenore, in helping her in having pain-free hours, in hearing Stephanie giggle, and in sharing a few snatches of good news with Nicole — despite all the bad stuff. Even in the worst *NOW* there were some things I was able to latch on to.

Most people can find some such moments if they look for them, even during tough times.

Tell yourself about the many times when you were competent, no matter what the subject; when you had fun and what those times were; when you felt decent, even good. It isn't your fault that life knocked you down. It's up to you to get back up, the way you did many times in the past. There have been times when you stumbled; focus your attention on the fact that you really did get back up.

And this leads to the second thing you can do if the NOW is very hard: recognize that you are a resilient person.

Even your difficult and painful moments can be an inspiration to you. I know this sounds strange, but look at it this way: each time you get knocked down and get up again, you have shown yourself how resilient you can be. Think of the rubber band or zipper. Neither of them can function without opposing tension. A rubber band can hold nothing together unless it is stretched outside its 'comfort zone'. You have been stretched to your limit and you have survived. Think of yourself as this rubber band. Yes, life has stretched you out, but you are a resilient person. The compassion you have received and the compassion you give others is part of your rubber band. See yourself as someone who faces difficult moments and finds a way to deal with them. This combination of focusing on the good things in your life, your strengths, and your capacity to get through stressful times and bounce back from mistakes will help you to be aware of yourself as someone quite able to rebound. And that awareness will help you to become even more resilient.

As you go through the day, notice and mark for future reference, times when you are bouncing back from adversity. If something goes wrong, don't focus on the fact that something went wrong; focus on how you overcame and managed it. Here's an example: instead of falling apart because your husband is no longer there to fix the broken screen door, you feel sad for the moment. Then you call the handyman. Or fix it yourself. This is a sparkling example of you rebounding. And again being in charge of your life.

Here's an example of something that entered *my* life: Sen. Ted Kennedy was diagnosed with a brain tumor. Shocking news for him and his family. But believe it or not, I became involved in his bad news because I chose to. I thought, 'Give or take a few months, he and I are the same age. If this disease could suddenly happen to him it could happen to me'. True enough. Also, not true enough.

Haven't you done something like this? You read about a famous person dying suddenly of a heart attack and you think, Ohmigod! When's the last time I had my cholesterol checked? This same thing could happen to me!

As we get older we notice that people our age and younger are dying. How, I ask myself, did I manage to escape thus far? Luck. Just luck. Maybe next month or next year I won't be this lucky.

But this is totally wrong. There is no reason to expect that next month or next year I will get a brain tumor or any other ailment. Why would I choose to think this, to live in the negative future, to do this to myself? And so I chose to stop it. Right that moment. I chose to return to the *NOW*. No more tumor; no more disease. The sun was shining. It was autumn and all was right with the world.

My inspiration for the change in thinking was Senator Kennedy himself, by the example he chooses to live. At great physical and emotional struggle, he willed himself to come to the Democratic Convention in the fall of 2008 in order to make a speech supporting Barack Obama. A few months after that he came to the Senate with his wife and two dogs, in order to cast a vote. He pulled himself back from a fearful future to a mindful present. He chose to live in the *NOW*. The emphasis is both on *chose to* and *NOW*. He might not be able to live a lot longer, but his future will be on his terms, not that of his disease.

Thirty-five years ago I frequently allowed myself to have catastrophic thinking. It didn't take much for me to take a relatively bad situation and turn it, in my mind, into a totally horrible situation, out of my control. I use the words 'allowed myself' because I eventually taught myself to stop thinking this way. I stopped *allowing* myself to think this way. I'm telling you this because there is almost nothing in your life that is a catastrophe. The only thing that would make it so is your *belief* that it is. There are many things in your life that seem catastrophic. Pull away from this thinking. You might not be in charge of your life right now, but you can be. And you will be. Live in the present.

The time has come to rediscover yourself. You have talents and interests. What are they? Are there things you've always wanted to do but haven't had the incentive to pursue?

But . . . I have been asked: What if you don't have kids or a well-developed talent? The answer is that everybody has something. Stay present and think of who you are. This requires a process of discovery that is well worth your time.

This is your opportunity. You are about to reinvent yourself. Your world has changed and you are going to find your new place in it. Look for clues as to what sparks your interest, makes you happy.

And don't forget the little things. Learn to love the fall; realize that in the depth of winter, spring will soon arrive. Notice the new leaves on the trees, the breeze on your face, the triumph of completing a Sudoku, or the purr of your cat. You will find that these little things are no longer little. They are life.

Think of the names of all the people you know, some old, some young. Realize that it is inevitable that some of them will die, no matter their age. But this isn't a cause for mourning. It just is. Think of an older relative who might die soon. No need here, either, to grieve in advance of his or her death. Instead, join their life and live in it by living in their *NOW*. Treasure every day she or he has with you, and these will be days of light you will remember for years.

The present, the *NOW*, is where you will live from this time forward. You will teach yourself that there is no need for emotional and mental suffering. You have already experienced the grief that was necessary; now it is time to rejoin your life which is already in progress, getting ready for living in the *NOW*.

Your future, the pleasant part of your future, wants to start right this minute. Let it.

Reinforcements:

- At the end of each day jot down things that were fulfilling and gave you pleasure. Try doing this on note cards and save the cards. Soon you will have a whole stack of positive moments to remember.

- On note cards, write times when you were resilient during the day or week. Keep these cards where you can easily access them. As your collection grows, look at it and understand that you are growing also. You are teaching yourself to be a resilient person capable of bouncing back from adversity.

- Stop at random times and ask yourself to find just one positive thing around you.

- Notice what it is that causes your endorphins to flow. What makes you happy? For instance, what parts of the newspaper do you read first; at which shelves in the bookstore do you linger? What sites do you visit on your computer? These are cues and clues to reinventing yourself. And reinventing yourself is exactly what you will begin to do.

STEP 7. START PRACTICING

You're ready to practice living in the NOW. You don't have to do everything at once, but you can do it a bit at a time. First comes practicing being fully aware of this moment, these surroundings, this person who is you right now—practicing what may be called mindfulness.

Begin by living in the *NOW* for 2 minutes at a time; then 5 minutes; then 10; 20; and then 30. Don't think that you can learn this technique (and technique is what it is) by suddenly *getting* it; you won't. It takes practice.

For those first two minutes, fixate on your life as it is in the present moment. Not in general, but right now. Think about where you are, sitting in a chair, for instance, reading a book. Think how this book might be ready to help you change your life, if you allow it to happen.

Notice the color of your walls, the pictures you put on these walls, the books on your shelves. Look out your windows and listen for sounds outside those windows. What do you hear? Birds? Children? Cars?

For these two minutes, there is no past filled with grief and no future filled with fear. You are who you are, and not who you were or who you will be. Allow yourself to become totally captured by the present moment. Imagine that you are in a warm welcoming blanket.

Once you've done this for many short bursts, you'll find this *NOW* is here for you if you start to find yourself getting caught in the painful past or the fearful future against your wishes. Practice yanking yourself back to the present moment when you start to be pulled into a negative place.

Practice making choices about when you want to visit the past, what you want to visit, and how you want to visit it. Are you going to spend a set amount of time remembering your loved one at a *happy* moment? Or a set amount of time remembering a *sad* moment? Make it your choice. The same with the future. Visit it to plan, but not to worry needlessly. Then come back to *NOW*.

Let me tell you something that will reinforce what I just said: I give talks related to this book. Recently, at one of these talks, someone asked me if I don't feel all grieved-out?

No, I replied. The grief hasn't all gone away. Anyone who says you get over it completely hasn't experienced it. The thread of pain will always be a part of your life.

I'll give you an example: I was walking down the street one day, thinking of almost nothing when thoughts of Stephanie suddenly popped into my head. I was overwhelmed. At the same time I was flabbergasted. Where the hell did this come from? I didn't want to avoid such thoughts, thinking that could be unhealthy, but I didn't want to dwell on them that moment. And so I decided to think about them later. Not just later, but tomorrow . . . at ten in the morning. I made an appointment with myself to think about her and to grieve about her at that time. But just as with any other kind of appointment, I made sure to keep it. If you don't keep it you won't believe yourself next time you make one.

Think about all the good things that are in your life right now. Think about any of your accomplishments, small or large. Think about your strengths and the ways you've been resilient. Think about good people in your life, relatives or friends; near or across the country.

Think about your interests. Try pursuing them again, but with the idea that they may broaden, deepen, or change in some way. As I said, before my grief came to me, I was interested in photography, mainly landscapes and animals. After I emerged from grief and came out the other side, I changed from nature photography to people, primarily homeless people that I met on the street. This gave photography new meaning for me and allowed me to discover that my real love was fellow human beings.

There might be a new interest for you to discover, or another facet of one you already know. You've given yourself permission to learn what any of these might be. Now take steps to try them out. Some will turn out to be paths you will want to stay on. Others will be dead ends. That's perfectly normal. You're *practicing* reinventing yourself in the world you have *NOW*. The practice will take you to where you want to be.

You are beginning to practice the other part of being in the *NOW*, broadening and deepening who you are, reinventing yourself to live in the world you have now. You don't have to set any big goals for accomplishment. Just notice what interests you and what you can do, and then try doing it.

Think of this: If you decided to learn to cook, play the piano, or speak French, it is obvious that none of these came automatically. Nor did they come without a misstep here and there. Living in the *NOW* is also a learned process. It won't come automatically; it will be a series of two steps forward, but expect also that there will be one step back. The good news is that you *will* get there.

Imagine that you are on an ocean liner, bound for Europe. You are on a cruise with your friends and loved ones. Everyone you care about is on board with you. Everything you could possibly need is on board also. Your stateroom is large and comfortable; the food is excellent and available day or night; the ocean is calm and the motion of the ship is just enough to make a gently rocking sensation.

You have left everything that has ever happened to you on the shore behind as soon as the ship left the dock. Some of these experiences were marvelous; some were devastating. But you realize that they are nevertheless all behind you. You have developed the ability to select which of these memories you will allow to rejoin you on the ship. You have decided that the pleasant memories may return at any time. But the unpleasant ones are left on the receding horizon; they may return only when you choose to have them visit, and even then for only as long as you wish them to remain.

You begin to think of your destination with pleasure. But soon you have other thoughts crowding in. Thoughts that other things might be in store for you. Unpleasant events have happened to you before the ship sailed and there is every reason to believe that they could happen again. And these thoughts of the feared future begin to cloud over the anticipation of your destination.

And so, as you sit on the deck with the warm glow of the setting sun bathing you in its warmth, you teach yourself to practice. You are here on your favorite ship in the middle of your favorite ocean with everything in life you need or could possibly want here with you. There is no reason to think of what you have left in your wake on that now distant shore. And you don't. Instead you make yourself focus on the voyage of this trip and this trip only.

When the negative thoughts of what might happen after you get off the ship crowd in on you, you push them away, realizing that you don't ever have to get off this ship. You let yourself relish the destination for what it is and the voyage for what *it* is.

Every day you will remember this cruise and by remembering you practice. You practice living this ship of your present life, leaving any unpleasant past behind you where it belongs; and you don't arrive at a fearful destination because you don't need to. For your future you choose to have nothing but warm thoughts of good things that lie in store.

And you practice, at first for 2 minutes a day; then 10, 20, then 30. You will eventually welcome these 30 minutes each day as your chosen means of calming your mind. They will become your favorite way of starting each day, or if you wish, the perfect way to end your day before bed.

Before disaster overtook you, you were a worthwhile, valuable and loving person. You will be again.

Reinforcements:

- Set times of the day when you will stop and be mindful of what is happening *NOW*. Notice the room you are in, the light in the room, the details, the view outside, the sounds you her, the smells and tastes you experience. At first, this might be just once a day, then twice, then more often.

- When you find your mind getting stuck in the past or the future, rein in back to the *NOW*.

- Take steps to follow up on the clues you've discovered about how you could reinvent yourself. Sign up for a class, go to a lecture, join an interest group, just to try them out. You don't have to find a new passion on the first try. The idea is to see what fits for you.

STEP 8. CROWD OUT THE NEGATIVES

You will by now have begun developing a *habit* that is so full of *NOW* that it crowds out the past and future. See yourself doing this in all of your daily life. This habit will have become as much of your existence as your ability to drive a car or eat lunch, and at least as important and necessary to your well-being. This newly acquired habit of *NOW* won't feel strange; it will be effortless. As a matter of fact, it will feel strange thinking any other way.

Crowd out the negatives, but leave room for the love you have felt and were given in the past — coupled with the hope that it will once more recur in the future — if you let it — by way of the *NOW*.

You cannot crowd out the negatives in your mind unless you first replace them with positive thinking. We are what we think. And we become *how* we think. We must populate our minds with thoughts that are designed to bring us upward into the light and not backward into dark places.

More than 55 years ago there was a book called the *Power of Positive Thinking* by Norman Vincent Peale.

These were some of his tenets:
- Expect the best and get it
- Believe in yourself and in everything you do
- Develop the power to reach your goals
- Break the worry habit and achieve a relaxed life
- Improve your personal and professional relationships
- Assume control over your circumstances
- Be kind to yourself

And this is the saying he was probably best known for:

Change your thoughts and you change the world.

Here is mine: change your thoughts of the painful past and the fearful future to the present and you will change *your* world.

In spite of the fact that the book sold over seven million copies, some people thought his advice was overly simplistic. It might be. But it works. Look at the sixth one: Assume control over your circumstances. It sounds like what I am advising about grief. And living in the *NOW* is certainly assuming control over the circumstances of this grief.

How can you fill up the rest of your mind with positives? Where will you find things to be positive about? Look at the list of seven, above. I will select three of them for you to use personally:

<u>Expect the best and get it</u>. How shall we define 'best'? This is an easy one. Letting go of the pain of the past and of the feared future, while holding on to the golden present is as best as it gets. Think of his first word, 'expect'. Living in the NOW won't fall into your lap. You will make it happen by *expecting* it will happen. And there is no doubt in the world that it will happen. The life you need to live will begin to appear. It won't be the same life but it will have the quality you want and need. Because you will *expect* it to happen.

<u>Break the worry habit and achieve a relaxed life</u>. Where is most of your worry coming from? From the feared future of course. Worry about you and your loved ones and your future. But soon you will teach yourself the idea of substitution. You will substitute worry about you with confidence that your life has just started to turn a corner. You might not be there yet, but you are sure on the right path; and you will substitute worry about your loved ones and your future with the knowledge that no one can predict the future. And there is absolutely no connection between anything bad that happened to you in the past and what will happen to you from now on.

<u>Be kind to yourself</u>. Oh, do you need it! And do you deserve it! Life has already been unkind and it's time for you to step in and ensure that the path ahead is serene.

Do something for your mind. Engage your jangling mind in a way that suits you, either up or down. You might want to stimulate it by reading a good book or watching an interesting movie. Or you might want to calm your mind by doing relaxation techniques or thru prayer, contemplation, or meditation (Appendix B). Set aside time each day for you and your pleasure, the same way as if you were making an appointment. But this is an appointment with yourself, for yourself.

Do something physical. Joining and using a health club can be a tremendous stress reliever. The same health club might have yoga lessons. You don't have to be in great shape to do either. Beginners are welcomed and nurtured. Believe me, it's hard to worry on a treadmill. Or you can exercise without joining a health club. You might find that in walking outdoors, or perhaps gardening, you become a part of nature and allow nature to become a part of you, exercising your body and finding a measure of tranquility.

The human brain is capable of holding only one thought at a time. If you fill your mind with positives, or at least neutrals, there will be no room for negatives. But think of this: if you fill your mind with 85% positives, you still are leaving room for 15% negatives. Crowd out the negatives by finding things to appreciate, but don't get exotic. Learn to love the mundane such as: why doesn't your bookshelf fall down? Because someone designed the supports. Cleverly. Admire the books that you put on those shelves. Some of them are probably worth reading a second time. Allow yourself to discover which they are.

Reinforcements:

- As soon as a negative thought comes into your mind, shift your focus to something immediate and positive. Immerse yourself in that *NOW* experience whether it be the beauty of a shaft of sunlight slicing thru the black clouds of a storm, or the sight of a small child running to greet her grandfather arriving at the airport. Accept every positive gift that comes your way, large or small.
- Try setting aside a 10 minute period each day for worrying. Select a time that would almost always be avail-

able to you. At that time which you have chosen, sit in a comfortable chair and allow worries to have your full attention; worry as much as you like during that time. If worries come up at other times, tell them they have to wait until your Worry Time comes around again. But until then focus on the positives of *NOW*.

- Try relaxation techniques. Try breathing in and out slowly from the diaphragm. (If this is hard for you to do, try it first while lying down on your stomach. That will force you to breathe from the diaphragm rather than the lungs.) Say a word or two, or a short phrase which has meaning to you, as you breathe in and out in a relaxed way. When you find which word or words work for you, keep using them. These words don't have to be explicitly spiritual, although they can be. You could breathe in "Courage" and breathe out "Peace." Or breathe in "I can" and breathe out "Do it." Or in . . . "God is" . . . and out . . . "with me."

- Try walking while saying your word or phrase to yourself. See whether you feel calmer by adding motion to the breathing and the repetitive phrase or whether you prefer to remain in one place.

- If the relaxation techniques work for you, try the next step: *meditation*. Perhaps this is a new concept to you. If it is, I have included a short, simple explanation and instruction in Appendix B which will introduce you to something that will help clear your mind. After you have tried it for a while, you might want to look into other long-established traditions. Some of these use mantras. A mantra is usually a word or phrase that you would think about while calming your mind, similar to the repetitive words or phrases used in the relaxation techniques. It is used to replace the chattering thoughts that occupy many of our minds and prevent clarity. You might, for example, think the word 'calm' as you slowly breathe in and the word 'relax' as you exhale. You will feel your body relaxing while sitting alone in a quiet space; but you can just as easily do the same while walking in the woods by yourself. You will teach yourself to relax even in motion. After you have said your mantra many times while meditating, you may find the simply thinking of that word or phrase calms you when you are in a stressful situation.

STEP 9. DO UNTO OTHERS

Reach out. Help someone else. At first, these might be just small gestures. Say hello to someone new. If you extend yourself and greet someone, you won't have time for your own negatives in that moment. Simply taking an interest in another person could mean a lot to them and will have the effect of lifting you out of yourself. You change the lens thru which you view life from that of grief to that of shared humanity.

Notice the goodness of people you hadn't noticed before. Is the person across from you on the train frowning because she is a grouch? Or could she be someone who is lonesome? You don't need to do anything more than simply recognizing this.

After some time, you may be ready to reach out to someone else who is grieving or in some kind of pain. Giving of yourself, helping others who are somehow in pain, getting beyond the 'me' orientation, will help you enormously.

At the appropriate time, introduce them to living in the *NOW*. You will find that helping someone else will lessen your pain.

Here's the challenge: You must have no *intention* that it will benefit you, in order for it to truly help you. Sounds like a contradiction, doesn't it? Here's how it works: It means that if you reach out to others to genuinely comfort them and empathize with them, the message then rebounds and helps the giver. But you must do it to help them, not you; otherwise, it won't help you at all.

When I offered my compassion to a friend whose child had died, there was no motive on my part that this would help me.

But as a result of my reaching out, the rebound occurred and I was greatly helped in dealing with my own grief, primarily because there was no intention on my part for gain.

When you think about it, *Do unto others* is the essence of applying living in the *NOW* to lessening your state of grief. It is all the way down at Step #9 because it is assumed that by this time you have learned – you have allowed yourself – to absorb *NOW* into your inner core and you have committed yourself to doing the absolute best for yourself that you possibly can. Only by coming out of your ME shell will you be able to achieve this.

Recognizing that the *cause* of the pain comes from the past, bring that forward to your present-day. Carry that further forward to helping someone else in their need.

My fiancée, Anne, and I have both suffered the loss of a spouse; Anne 24 years ago and I more recently. We have this thread, this common experience of having loved and then having our loved one die. This gives us a deep sense of connection. And it gives us a recognition that we need to reach out to others who are in pain, just as others reached out to us when we were in the depths.

Anne's son, Tom is presently in medical school. Losing his father when he was a small boy is now making him a more understanding and compassionate doctor-to-be for his patients. Because it is part of his tapestry, he is not afraid to be present to others when they are afraid or in pain.

This is another example of controlling what you can, walking away from that which you cannot. Using your personal knowledge of pain to connect with others, and transforming the pain of your grief into something used to heal. And when you help them heal, you will both become whole.

Reinforcements:
- Start noticing other people. Think of how you might interpret expressions on their faces and the things they say and do in a way that opens the possibility of their having good intentions.

- Smile and say hello to someone in an office corridor or on the street instead of just passing them by.
- Be open to having a conversation with someone you meet for the first time. Try to learn as much about them as you can by asking questions. Don't ask what they do for a living; it will color your opinion. Instead, ask what they are interested in.
- Reach out to someone you haven't talked to in a while or whom you don't know well. Don't allow yourself one of those 'you owe me a phone call'.
- Consider joining a group or organization which has the helping of others as its function.
- Simply reach out to another person who might have need of what you have to offer.

STEP 10. BECOME ADDICTED TO NOW

You will find that your habit has developed into almost an 'addiction' to *NOW*. This is one of the better addictions. By now you're really hooked. If you have ever smoked and given it up, you will realize how difficult it is to leave something behind, even something that isn't good for you.

And you'll never again leave the *NOW* behind. It will have become as easy and natural to you as breathing. The idea of living again in the past or future will seem outlandish to you. So outlandish, that you simply won't do it.

Here are examples of the new you, living in the *NOW*:

A. You are 55 years old and have been with the same company for 30 of those years, giving them the no need for you to leave living behind, and you decide that you are going to take charge of the rest of your life.

You begin living in the *NOW* and leave the past behind. Just as valuable, you detach from the future also and stop fearing that which hasn't happened. You are not going to die because you lost your job. By living in the present you will clear your mind and by doing so will be able to find another position, as unlikely as that might seem at the moment. You are living right this moment; no longer yesterday and no longer tomorrow. Only *NOW*. This is the only time that matters.

B. Your dog has died and you are disconsolate. A few months go by and you remember what you have learned about living in the *NOW*. After rereading the Ten Steps, you proceed from #1 to #9. Then, once you have reached this point, you enter #10, where you are right this moment. Realizing that life must go on, even though your dog's has ended, you take the only reasonable step open to you. You go to a shelter and see if you can find another dog. Not as great as your other one perhaps, but still someone who needs you and someone you need. And life does go on.

C. Last Saturday, you attended a dinner party at a friend's house and made an egregious error. You called his wife *Mary*, which was the name of his first wife, whom you knew quite well, not the current one. You were tremendously embarrassed, even though they both laughed and said there was no problem. But in your mind you were sure that the error was virtually unforgivable, and that you would never again be invited back.

After you returned home, you thought that without realizing it, you had slipped into the old habit of reliving that event and therefore living in the past. You immediately shifted the gears in your mind and brought yourself back to *NOW*. The dinner party from Saturday became meaningless in the light of today, Tuesday, as you understood that today was wonderful and you didn't need Saturday and its perceived pain. Nor did you need the future idea that you would never be invited back. If you were invited back, that would be fine; if you weren't, you would survive. You would, at the very least, have learned the depth of this relationship with your friend.

In fact, you could take the initiative and invite them to your house, showing that you weren't going to allow your past mistake to be a barrier to your maintaining a friendship.

D. Your older brother has died. Your only sibling. But now a year has passed and you have decided that it was your brother who died, not you. There is no need for both of you to leave living behind, and you decide that you are going to take charge of the rest of your life. you remember your brother with love and you honor that memory by going on with your life.

You begin living in the NOW and leave the past behind. Just as valuable, you stop worrying about the future also, and you stop fearing that which hasn't happened.

✦
ACKNOWLEDGEMENTS

It is easier to think of the contributions others have made to me and to this book than it is to adequately write this, which is essentially a written thank you. They all gave much and asked for nothing in return. A rare commodity.

A thank you to my cousin and fellow author Madelyn Cain (look for her on Amazon.com). Her countless emails, encouragement, critiques and reading and rereading earlier drafts of the book were and are of immense value.

My daughter and first editor, Nicole, was incredibly helpful with her suggestions and marvelous rewrites that encouraged me to keep going even when I felt it was beyond difficult. She is my daughter first but my confidante every step of the way thereafter.

Early on, Carol Lauhon encouraged me to develop the self-help aspect of my book, and for that I thank her. Other friends, also at Lake Street Church in Evanston, Illinois, heard one of my talks on the book then offered advice and encouragement that both raised the quality of the book and sustained me with their words.

Tom Nagy, Ph.D., took the time from his busy practice as a clinical psychologist and an adjunct professor at Stanford to read an earlier draft of this book. His useful insights, including his suggestion that we provide practical exercises for people trying to live in the Now, have enriched the book.

A thank you also to the wonderful Bernie Siegel, M.D., the author of *Love, Medicine and Miracles*. It was my miracle that he agreed to read my book and then a sequel to this miracle when he offered advice as to how it could be improved; advice, of course, that I accepted with gratitude.

And my gratitude to Earl Grollman for his support and belief in this book and the beneficial effect it could and would have on the thousands who enter the world of grief each day. His note to me appears on the back cover and is something I appreciate and treasure well beyond my ability to express. Earl is the author of *Living When A Loved One Has Died* and 26 other books.

Finally, to my wife, Anne Berenberg, without whom this book would have essentially remained in its original form of memoir and without being of benefit to those who need it most. If she were not a clinical psychologist she would surely have been an editor of astounding ability at a major publishing firm.

Anne spent hour upon hour with me as we bounced ideas off one another, polishing and burnishing until every comma was mutually agreed upon. She read and edited every page, and then again, and then again for each of the final drafts. Her passion for perfection drove me to also do no less. The changes she suggested were usually met with initial skepticism on my part, and just as usually accepted and incorporated.

Her insights and her depth of experience as a clinical psychologist are especially apparent in the comments at the ends of chapters and in the Ten Steps, which she co-authored.

This book is as much Anne's product as it is mine.

APPENDIX A

LENORE'S JOURNAL

SECOND SURGERY

And there we were, preparing for surgery, same hospital, same floor, eight days after the first.

These are some of Lenore's thoughts, from her journal:

That day, I waited in my room at Lake Forest hospital for the gurney. Even though they gave me something like Valium, I could feel the anxiety growing. How I hated that feeling that makes you so helpless! And what made it really bad is that they had already given me drugs to calm me down. That meant that the anxiety was going to be with me, pills or not. It was both scary and depressing.

"I don't mind having surgery as long as they knock me out." How many times have I said that?

It's true that I insisted on being completely knocked out. But it isn't true that I never minded. Jack believed it because I wanted him to believe it. I didn't want him to know how scared I am. He's going to be really surprised if he ever reads what I have written here.

I'm the sort of person who wants to get something over with. If I've got something negative coming up I don't like to put it off.

I remember that Dr. Brill started to speak to me but I don't even recall that he finished the sentence because I drifted off and didn't wake up again until I was back in my room.

When the anesthetic wore off, I remember I had a pain in my left arm pit but didn't have pain in my right breast. I did have pain in my right shoulder blade, strangely enough.

Because I'm a naturally curious person I wanted to see the wound sites. However, both my right breast and my left arm-pit were wrapped in serious bandages. Jack was sitting on a chair near the foot of the bed. He asked me how I was feeling and of course I said, I'm ok. I had a feeling that this isn't the first time he asked me the same question. I was feeling very sad at the time and don't know why. Probably because I had simply had too many surgeries too close to each other.

That night after Jack left, I lay there in my room and started thinking. Thinking at night was both a blessing and a curse. It's a blessing because I had the time to think without interruption from the nurse or from Jack or from anyone else. But it's also a curse because the worst time to think negative thoughts is late night alone in hospital. I started focusing on my fears. I had no idea where I would go from here. Would this be the end of it? Was I starting a downward spiral? I was afraid of a lot of things, and they weren't neuroses because they were quite possible, quite real.

I am never afraid of death itself. I am afraid of suffering. I am afraid of loss of control. But the fear of death did consume me when I thought of separation from my family: my daughters, my son, and Jack. And most of all it is the fear of never being able to see my first grandchild. I never knew when a grandchild might come along, but then I never knew when I might die either. As if this weren't enough, I had radiation and chemo waiting in the background. I still didn't know what to expect from either of these.

The fear of suffering obsessed me. I made everyone I spoke to promise that I would never suffer. I talked to the doctor, the nurses, and Jack. They all had their own areas of time. I needed the nurses to promise me I wouldn't suffer during my stay in hospital. The doctor had to promise me for any time that I am in his care. And Jack, poor Jack, had to promise me that I would never ever suffer at any time for the rest of my life. He promised, and I believed him, but I'm not sure why.

Fear of loss of control is almost as bad. When I start the chemo or the radiation, how will I know if I'll lose control of my bladder or my anus; how do I know that my legs won't fail me, how do I know that my brain will still function?

It's easy to be logical and even cheerful in the daytime, at home. But lying in a hospital bed after surgery at night there's no logic and there's nothing cheerful about it. The night nurses came in for tests and to check on me. Most people complain about this fact of hospital life, but at that time I almost welcomed it because it broke my negative chain of thought.

The nurses on all three shifts were terrific. They were compassionate, knowledgeable, and just plain wonderful. One of them had at turban on and I could tell she had no hair underneath. On the second day I got up my nerve and asked her if she is taking chemo. She said, quite cheerfully, yes I am, I have breast cancer. I, of course, asked her if she is scared. She said she was at first but not any more. She said they caught it early and she felt she had beaten it. This did quite a lot to raise my spirits, because they caught my cancer early also.

The pain was quite severe, but only infrequently. And in any case, it is managed quite well by the nursing staff and the doctors. I've always had a fear of pain and I didn't hesitate to tell them this. Since they knew where I stood, they always reacted quickly and well. I never suffered unduly.

On the day after surgery, Dr. Brill came in to see how I am doing. By this time my armpit had started to burn. I told the doctor this and tried not to let the concern show in my voice. He assured me that it is normal and if anything, it is going to burn even more as the days went by because the skin is starting to pull against the staples. Believe it or not this made me feel better. Like everyone else, fear of the unknown overwhelms everything. As long as I knew that everyone else is likely to get a burning sensation in the armpit after the surgery, I felt better.

SECOND SURGERY

From Lenore's journal:

On the 22nd of March my radiation started. I had horrible anxiety. What were they going to do to me? How could I

*survive all this? I had read of radiation burns when some-
one made a mistake and the patient got terribly disfigured.
I don't know where I got that from. Maybe some movie.
Anyway, Jack and I went to the radiation department at
Lake Forest Hospital that day and went in to see the radiation oncologist, Dr. Imperiale, a kindly man who took great
care to explain everything to us in great detail. Strangely
enough, this time I heard and understood everything. I think
that once I got past the first horror of hearing the bad news
about my cancer from Dr. Brill, I developed a mental cal-
lous. With my mind quieted down somewhat I was able to
focus on my new path. The radiation was to take place five
times a week for six weeks; Saturdays and Sundays off.*

*The whole thing sounded logical to me and Jack and I
agreed to move forward with it. My apprehension, it turned
out, was unnecessary.*

*The radiation itself is a no-brainer. I lay down on a table on
my back. The physicist determined what was needed and gave
the instructions to the radiation therapists who very carefully
positioned the machine and turned on an aiming light which
drew a target area by means of a grid outlined by shadows.
They set the machine for the correct dosage and fired away.
It is almost disappointing. It lasted as long as an x-ray and
had the same feeling: nothing. The difference is that they followed the same procedure three more times, each time moving the big canister that emits the radiation in a higher arc.
They needed to zap me from different angles. All in all, the
whole thing took probably no more than five minutes once
the physicist had completed her work. The crew explained to
me that I could expect the same thing every time I came. The
only feeling I would notice would be that the radiation had
a cumulative effect and as time went by I would start to feel
more and more tired, though nothing terrible.*

*Weeks later, I agreed with what they said, but at the same
time wondered if they hadn't told me, would I have still felt
tired? It's good to be forewarned but sometimes we can feel
something that isn't really there. At times I do this when I
read about the side effects on drug labels.*

*While I was doing the radiation thing, Jack stayed behind
to talk to . . . interview. . . .Dr. Imperiale. Even though he had*

already decided on the Brachytherapy he thought it would be a good idea to learn about external beam radiation. The doctor of course thought it was the best therapy and told him he should seriously consider it. I don't think Jack came away enthused about it simply because he couldn't get past the concept of external beam radiation passing through the other organs to reach the prostate.

After I started the radiation therapy we felt it would be a good idea to talk to the man who would be directing my next area of treatment, the chemotherapy. I had always said for years that if I ever got cancer I would never go through chemo. But now that I was faced with the decision, I realized that I wasn't so sure and that I was reserving judgment until I talked to the doctor. The fact is I said this but didn't believe it. I was scared to do it, but more scared not to. I was afraid of the vomiting and having my hair fall out. But neither happened. My hair got thinner, but it was so thick to begin with that it is hardly noticeable. As to being nauseated, I learned about a miracle drug, Zofran. This plus another one I got, Compazine, were given in my IV before the start of each chemo to counter any possibility of nausea.

Dr. Patel came into the room and introduced himself. He was a small man from India with a very pleasant voice and manner. He immediately instilled calm and confidence in me. It took almost no time before Jack was asking him about his home town in the south of India and then telling the doctor of the trip Jack and Adam took there a few months before. I began to feel very aggravated; Jesus Christ! I thought, we were there, after all, to discuss my disease and treatment, not to talk about travel and geography. But soon enough, Dr. Patel steered the conversation to me and my problem.

He told us that I had infiltrating ductal carcinoma. Infiltrating is self-explanatory; ductal, he said, means that the cancer had infiltrated a milk duct; and that any word ending in "oma" means a mass or tumor. Luckily, mine was Stage 1, which is the earliest possible form. The cure of cancer is almost always related to time: discover it early and many, if not most, are curable. Catch them late and few survive. Once the cells spread, or metastasize, they are beyond the reach of modern medicine. I felt relieved to hear that it was

Stage 1. For the first time I could see the end of the tunnel and hope emerged that I would beat this thing.

I sat there listening about the chemo, thinking about the surgery and the radiation and couldn't help feeling that I was being sucked into a whirlpool from which I might never emerge. I saw myself as a human yo-yo, down with the first news of the cancer; up with the hope I got from Dr. Patel; then down again the more we discussed the chemo. I felt like saying, "Why Me?", but I wasn't going to fall into that trap. I realized that I was embarking on a journey on which so many had preceded me. I had read about them and heard about them for years but never entertained the idea that I would be one of them. Who among us could imagine being in the same spot one day? Certainly I couldn't. Others might be sick; they can be poor or helpless. But not me. When we are young we are bulletproof. As we get older we understand we never had the shield and sooner or later we become fearful when we realize that anything can happen to any one of us.

In spite of past thoughts that I would never agree to chemo if I ever was diagnosed with cancer, I decided to go with it. I felt it would be foolish not to, and so we started the overlap, chemo before even finishing the radiation. It bothered me a lot that I was still doing the radiation when I started the chemo. Radiation five times a week and then chemo twice a month on the 1st and 8th days. The good news, if you could call it that, was that the radiation would end in a few weeks and then I would have only the chemo left to do from then until November.

As I left the hospital after my last radiation on the 5th of May, I thought: this was my own personal Cinco de Mayo; my own day of independence. The surgeries and the radiation were behind me. Two kinds of procedures down, one to go. Chemo.

MORE DOCTORS: THIS TIME FOR JACK

From Lenore's journal:

I really wanted to go to Seattle with Jack for his Brachytherapy. After all he'd been through with me I would have felt guilty if I couldn't go. The biggest problem was that we'd be gone in the midst of one of my chemo treatments. But a secondary problem was that I also didn't want to go to chemo alone. I had a number of people who volunteered to go with me but at that stage it was Jack and Jack only that I wanted. And I know he felt the same about me going with him to Seattle.

I asked my best friend, Rosemary Cibelli about it. Rosum was my constant companion on my Saturday shopping excursions with Stephanie. We would go anywhere and buy anything. What we bought wasn't important. The shopping was the main game. One week we'd be at Saks, the next at K-Mart. The great thing about Rosum was that she was as nuts as I was. No matter what crazy outing I suggested, she thought it was reasonable.

When I asked if she thought I was being silly about wanting Jack with me at chemo, she seemed almost startled. "Not at all," she said. "Why wouldn't you want him to be there? Who better to have with you at a time like this than Jack? Except me of course."

The fact was that after thinking about it, I could have been just as comfortable having Rosum with me as Jack, but since chemo was done during the day, her job ruled her out. She asked me how I am going to solve this.

I didn't know how to solve it. So we asked Dr. Patel. He said that we'd be gone less than a week and if I shifted my chemo from one week to the next it wouldn't make any difference. Naturally we accepted the offer and scheduled our trip to Seattle for Jack's surgery.

After the surgery, we went back to the motel and Jack went to bed and watched television and read. He was feeling good except that every so often he would have to urinate. The problem was that when he got into the bathroom he couldn't. It was very frustrating for him. The other problem was that he would try to go to sleep and his legs became so restless that he couldn't get comfortable and so didn't sleep. I told him he should take a pain killer called Darvocet which his doctor prescribed and which we had filled on the way back from the hospital. But Jack was very stubborn and was not a pill-taker. He resisted doing this but I felt it was simply a matter of time before he came around to my way of thinking. He did. Within 20 minutes of finally taking one you could see him visibly relaxing and shortly after that he fell asleep.

We went back to the hospital the next day so that they could check out Jack's condition and after that we went back to the motel. The day after that we returned to Chicago, both Jack and the doctors being satisfied that he was free from complications.

The flight home was easy, but I'm glad we waited the extra day. Leaving the day before would have caused more anxiety for both of us.

Well, finally 1993 ended. What a year! It started out a nothing, but all the stuff after that, Jack's cancer and my cancer.

My chemo ended in November. I hated going there, I hated being there and I hated the aftereffects. I hated the chemo. So wouldn't you think I would have a party when it ended? No. I didn't have a party. I was scared. My crutch was gone. I felt like my life support was gone. The chemo was protecting me from the evil in my body. I felt like I was out at the end of the plank, and there was no water in the pool. I had Jack, but at a time like this you feel alone.

It was a terrible feeling because it isn't supposed to be this way. I told Jack about it and to my surprise he understood what I meant. I don't know why, but I was afraid he'd laugh. I felt anyone would laugh at me being afraid to end the chemo. I was embarrassed to tell anyone else.

In February 1994, we joined the Cancer Wellness Center. I didn't want to. I don't see any point to support groups. But Jack wanted to join and I said that I'd go with him. The fact was, I think Jack wanted to join for my benefit not his. Anyway, we joined. They were a nice bunch of people. But if you're in a fragile state of mind, it can go either way. You can either get a great deal of support from the group that will make you feel wonderful or you can be in a group, as we were, in which a lot of people become your close friends, and then die. If someone in the group happened to be in the hospital or otherwise laid up, the group always made a telephone call to them at the end of the meeting. At the very first meeting we made a telephone call to someone named Sue. She was in the hospital having a bone marrow transplant. She couldn't have visitors and was delighted to have phone calls. The people in the group not only called her once a week from the meeting but also made individual calls from home. When they said they were a support group, they weren't kidding.

After a few months, it got to the point that Jack and I felt we really knew Sue, even though we never met her. Then, one day she showed up at the meeting. She had a baseball cap on to cover her bald head and a surgical mask over her face. This was to prevent any sort of infection after having the bone marrow transplant. She peered out at us through eyes behind glasses, and her eyes were the only thing that we could see of her entire face. About a month after that, she came to the meeting without cap or mask and we were startled to find out that she was Japanese. You would think that we would be able to tell Japanese eyes from Caucasian, but we never did. She was a wonderful person and we became very friendly with her until about four years later when she died. Another friend and I were with her the night before she died at Northwestern hospital. We bought her a teddy bear at the gift shop. When we went in it was apparent she was unconscious. So we simply put the teddy bear near her face. After a minute her hand reached up and felt the teddy bear, then she pressed it close to her cheek, and smiled. It was the last we ever saw of her, but it was a wonderful way to remember her.

The rest of 1994 was pretty much uneventful.

In January of 1995, Jack needed to go back to Seattle for a checkup with Dr. Ragde. Adam asked if he could go along and Jack immediately agreed. I felt this was a mistake but said nothing. Adam at this point was a non-worker, a heavy drinker, and a drug user. Which drugs he used were unknown to us but nothing would have surprised me. Seattle was ok but then they went to Vancouver and in spite of many precautions on Jack's part to prevent such a thing, Adam managed to get drunk. I felt sorry for Jack.

By April of 1996 we knew the breast cancer had been beaten. As much as you could ever say that cancer has been beaten. I desperately wanted to get my Portacath taken out. *At the same time I was understandably afraid. What if it came back and I had to have it reinserted? But I also couldn't stand the negative thinking. I had to prove to myself that I had to have the confidence to go on living. I went ahead.*

The doctor wanted to remove it under local anesthetic but I wouldn't hear of it. Jack was unhappy because he always regarded anesthesia as more dangerous than surgery, but I didn't care. I wanted to be knocked out. I just didn't want to be aware. So I did it my way. General anesthetic. It was great. When I woke up the port was gone and the pain was managed with Vicodin. No problem.

In September of that year Jack went to Kenya on a photo safari. He wanted me to go but I had no interest in the heat and the bugs. When he got back he said there were no bugs to speak of and the temperature was in the 70s. I don't care though. I didn't want to go. Besides, maybe he wasn't telling the truth.

". . . . THIS NEW BLACK FLAG ON OUR HORIZON."

Excerpts from Lenore's journal:

Everything was going along swimmingly until March of 1997. On the 19th, I got a terrific pain in the right side of my rib cage and couldn't imagine what it could be from. Jack, who loves to diagnose such things, couldn't figure it out either. The problem was that there didn't seem to be anything in that area other than my lung. I just chalked it up to another weird happening in my life. I took a pain pill and hoped it would go away the next day. It didn't. Jack wanted me to go to the doctor and have it checked out, his answer to everything. My answer was that I didn't want to see another doctor if I didn't have to. After all, it was just a pain and not life threatening.

On the second day the pain seemed to increase as the day wore on. It was sharp, as if someone was sticking a dagger in my side. But I wouldn't give in. I could see Jack was worried but I had to think of myself. I'm the one who had the pain and I'm the one who had to see the doctor. Maybe. Going would have made him feel better, but not me. I knew in my heart that the pain would be gone soon and even if no explanation for it were found, I didn't care.

It isn't just the pain. I was having a tough time breathing. It was hard to take a deep breath and I am not sure if that was because deep breaths increased the pain or that I was simply unable to take a deep breath. This worried me and made me think of lung cancer. I even considered stopping smoking. But I couldn't. It drove Jack and Nicole right up the wall, but again, they weren't the ones with the addiction. Jack quit about 30 years ago and I keep telling him there's nothing more obnoxious than an ex-smoker.

At the end of the third day, the 21ˢᵗ, I finally caved in. By now the pain killers weren't doing anything and I got out of breath walking across the room. My side hurt so much that it wasn't that hard to concede defeat. Late in the day Jack drove me to the ER at Lake Forest Hospital. I had been in this hospital so many times in the past that Jack jokingly referred to the Lenore Cain Wing. When we checked in I tried to keep a brave front but it was tough. We probably didn't wait too long but it seemed like hours especially when we were filling out forms.

The doctor in charge that night came in and listened and thumped asked me to take deep breaths which of course I couldn't do. Finally he said that it is possible it is lung cancer but he didn't think so. He thought it might be a blood clot. You have no idea how relieved I was. There was no way I could really deal with lung cancer; the survival rate is terrible. But a blood clot was something else. I didn't know what caused it but it didn't matter. It sounded like something we could take care of. He told me that he is sending me to x-ray to see what was going on. I was only too happy to comply since I wanted to get rid of this thing and also because x-rays are easy enough.

The doctor returned and told us that he had just looked at the films of my chest and they confirmed his suspicions. It isn't lung cancer; it is a blood clot. I can't tell you how happy this made me. Jack asked what would be done to

*correct this and the doctor said he was putting me on a
blood thinner called Coumadin. It was only a matter of
time before the clot was dissolved and the pain would be
gone.*

*But then he said this wasn't addressing the problem. Where
did the clot come from and why? This hadn't occurred to either one of us but it seemed a reasonable question. Almost
by reflex the doctor wanted me to quit smoking, saying that
even though this probably didn't cause the clot, it made the
whole thing worse. As soon as he said it probably didn't
cause it, I stopped listening.*

*He scheduled me for a CT scan the next day and I went
home, filling my Coumadin prescription on the way. I was
feeling better already, knowing that help was on the way and
also content that the CT would locate the root of the problem and possibly prevent something worse from happening.*

*The next morning we went back to Lake Forest for the
test and that afternoon Dr. Patel called. Jack spoke to him
and when he put down the phone I asked what was wrong.*

*"That was Dr. Patel," Jack replied, "and he said he has
bad news and good news."*

"Give me the bad news first," I said.

*"I'll give you both at once. The blood clot was caused by a
tumor on one of your ovaries. The good news is that it can't
be very old since it wasn't there in November, according to
Dr. Shewitz, I think he feels that the problem is correctable."
Dr. Shewitz was my gynecologist in whom I had the greatest
confidence.*

*I could feel an instant knot in my stomach. I didn't know
how much more of this I could take. As far as I was concerned I had beaten the breast cancer and now a tumor on
an ovary! Had the breast cancer spread? If so, it was the
worst possible news. It would mean that it had metastasized
and was spreading who knows how far?*

"How is it correctable?"

*"Surgery. He made an appointment for us to see Dr. Beck
tomorrow," Jack replied. "He's a surgeon and Dr. Patel
seems to think he knows what he's doing."*

*"Is this terrible news?" I asked, trying not to let my voice
show how scared I am.*

"Doesn't look like it," he answered. "Since it's new I'm guessing it's small and it will just be one more hurdle to get over."

We were both very good at protecting the other so I didn't know how much I should believe. But I decided to believe him totally since I didn't like thinking otherwise.

The next day we went to Dr. Beck's office, which he shares with Dr. Shewitz. Shortly after he started speaking I gained complete confidence that I was in good hands. To this day he remains one of my heroes. Dr. Beck appeared to be the sort of doctor who judges what patients really want to know and tells them accordingly. I don't know how he was reading me since he spoke primarily to Jack. He told it straight out.

"Is this a very new tumor?" Jack asked.

"Hard to say," the doctor replied. "Dr. Shewitz saw nothing there late last year when you were in and now the damned thing is there. I have to assume it's new."

"Can we also assume that it's small and controllable?"

At that point I detected the smallest hesitation on his part. But then I think he made his decision that we wanted to hear everything.

"I don't have any idea if it's controllable, but it's not that small. The tumor is 8cm."

"How big is that in inches?" I asked.

"It looks like it's a little more than three inches in diameter," he replied.

I am startled. Three inches in diameter would make it about the size of my fist. How could it be that large in such a short time and no one knew it? I am also getting the feeling that he is regarding this whole thing as a grave situation. He didn't say so in so many words, but the look on his face didn't seem too optimistic. I am afraid to ask. I needn't have worried: Jack asked.

"What's the prognosis?"

"Depends on what we find. We need to do a complete hysterectomy. I'd like to do it as soon as possible. I think this thing is a fast grower and there's nothing to be gained by waiting."

"When can you do it?"

"I could do it in the morning. Dr. Shewitz could assist me. Is that all right with you?"

This time he addressed the question to me. I nodded yes. There was no way I wanted to wait around any longer than that for surgery. If we're going to do it, let's do it now.

"Okay," he said, "tomorrow it is. I know that you've been to Lake Forest before so they'll have your records. But I'll want a new blood draw so I'll order that right away."

After the surgery, Dr. Beck came out to see Jack and told him that I tolerated the surgery well and that the tumor was the size he thought. He said that there were a few more very small tumors in areas near the ovary but he got them out. He also said that the other ovary isn't affected. That afternoon Dr. Beck stopped in to see how I am doing and told me where we went from there. He said the diagnosis was Stage III-C Ovarian Cancer and that Dr. Patel would discuss the chemo that we would need to do to beat this thing. They reinserted a Portacath during the surgery for just this purpose. They also put in what's called a Greenfield filter because they were afraid that pieces of the clot might break off due to the Coumadin. I couldn't get it out of my head that Dr. Beck didn't look optimistic about this.

Complications developed. The filter needed to be repositioned; the Portacath wasn't functioning correctly, and I was in the hospital 9 days. I had heard people being in a hospital this long, but never dreamed it would happen to me.

SUICIDE

Excerpts from Lenore's journal:

He is dead. My youngest, my baby, my Adam is dead. Thank God no one said it is all for the best or I would have hit them.

He had his problems and we had them with him. The drugs, the alcohol, the lack of friends — and those he did have weren't the best. No ambition. Using us and our feelings for him to move through the world without working.

That damned Cori, with her weird story to the police. Whoever heard of being terrified by your boyfriend and then going to bed with him and then calling the police hours later? No one who was telling the truth, that's who. And all the time he spent in jail she wouldn't change her story because she said her parents wouldn't let her. I don't believe her reason for not changing her story, but if I did believe it, it was just as bad. She isn't the sort of person I would have chosen as my life's companion, but then Adam wasn't that fussy. He got what he wanted: food, sex and shelter. And she got what she wanted: someone who said he loved her.

I generally followed Jack's lead in how we dealt with Adam. We discussed things; I had my input which he respected, but in the end I usually agreed with his take on each situation. With one exception. I am absolutely furious about what he did at Gurnee Mills, having Adam arrested. That was humiliating and arrogant and treacherous. He humiliated both Adam and me; he was arrogant to think that he could do that without consulting me; and it meant he turned his back on his own son.

Adam's suicide was the most shattering thing in my life. Before that I think it must have been the day Stephanie was born and we found out she had Down Syndrome. I loved her completely but I was shattered. But this was so much different. At least Stephanie is alive. They always say that the worst thing you could imagine is to lose a child. But I think people say this in the hope that it will never happen, and if they say it then maybe it won't happen. No one, including me, could ever imagine it would happen. And then it did. Actually, as bad as I feel, I feel worse for Jack. I can't imagine what he went through, finding Adam in the garage that way. I think about it and I sometimes think I know what it must have been like, but then I realize that I will never know the feeling and I don't want to know.

He died on Sunday and we had the funeral on Wednesday, to give people in California and other places time to come in. It was a beautiful funeral. Adam was cremated and we had the urn with his ashes on a table at the front of the room surrounded by about 50 photos of him in various stages of his life. We had a minister from the Unity Church conduct the ceremony and then about 10 people got up and said nice things about Adam. The minister recited the 23rd Psalm but changed it from 'my' to 'your'. He turned to the urn containing Adam's ashes and said, "The Lord is your shepherd, you shall not want, etc." Jack and Nicole and I wrote something also but none of us could read it and had friends do it for us.

This whole experience made Jack and me bitter about two things: psychiatrists and the Mormon Church. Adam was living at the Elgin State Hospital in the care of supposedly accomplished psychiatrists. They felt that he not only was capable of making home visits but had scheduled him for permanent discharge, saying he was essentially cured. None of them saw the suicide coming. But that's why they're in business. It seems to me that if they couldn't recognize this in advance, what was it they're doing anyway?

I was very angry with the Mormon Church. When he died three people from the church showed up. Even Cori came. I was surprised she had the nerve to show her face, but I suppose guilt overcame shame.

I sometimes wonder if one of the reasons he committed suicide was because of my cancer. He might have assumed that I was going to die and just didn't want to deal with it; he didn't want to be here when it happened. I have no way of knowing, but I hope this isn't one of his reasons. Things like this are tough enough without having to guess someone else's motives.

After he died, we went back to trying to live a normal existence as best we could. Thank God we had Stephanie and Nicole. I keep thinking what would have happened if Adam had been our only child? We decided to tell Stephanie nothing for the time being, and in the end, we never told her, we didn't have to.

If Nicole and Larry have a baby it would sure make me happy. I think people assume that my feelings on this are that I want a replacement for Adam, a ridiculous thought. First of all, nothing could replace him. And second, I had these feelings long before Adam died.

I just want to be a grandmother.

END IN SIGHT

Excerpts from Lenore's journal:

January 1999. I'm feeling sorry for myself again. A month ago my counts were dropping like a rock. Even the doctor was impressed that my numbers went down 80% in two months. Then why do I feel so bad? So tired I can hardly move. No interest in doing anything. Can't find any incentive to do anything. I feel completely wrung out.

This is pretty much what we talked about at that time:

"I don't know what to do," I said.

Jack looked quizzical. "About what?"

"About me. I'm tired all the time. I was tired when my counts were high and now that they're dropping I'm still tired. What do you make of it?"

"Nothing to be concerned about," he replied. "With all the stress you've had it's only normal to be tired. That and the Herceptin and the chemo. You're lucky you're not more tired than you are. But we're going to see Dr. Patel on Thursday. He'll probably think of something to help."

I loved the way he lied to me. Sometimes I even believed him. Maybe I usually believed him. Even when I knew he was lying. It was easier.

"You're tired because your blood count is way down," Dr. Patel said. "We have to get it up."

"How do we do that?" Jack asked.

"With a blood transfusion."

"What'll that do?"

"Giving Lenore more red blood cells. That's where the oxygen is. That's why she's so tired. Lack of oxygen in her blood. The cells in her body are starving."

Made sense to me. I didn't ask why my red blood cells were so low. I didn't want to ask. Something was causing it and Jack didn't ask either. He might have asked if I hadn't been there. So he probably had a reason not to ask. Maybe he already knew.

Something bad was going on here. All the good news of December seemed to be washed away in January. And the funny thing was that no one had said anything about bad news. I just felt it in my bones.

A few days later I got the transfusion. Even before I went to bed I felt better. But the next morning I didn't feel much more energetic. And that was as good as it got. A little better, but not much better.

And then in March, the pain started to come. It was what I dreaded the most. Dr. Patel prescribed morphine patches which I put on my arm and totally controlled the problem. In spite of the fact that I had told Jack many times that I was afraid of suffering, not dying, there was always this feeling of not knowing what was going on, and virtually living in a whirlpool. Frequently, I wanted to know exactly what was going on, and at the same time I really didn't

But the pain was a sign of things to come. I told Jack I didn't like the way this thing was going.

"I don't see a big problem here," he said. By this time his responses were getting thin and neither of us believed them. At least I didn't. "What's your biggest concern?"

"The numbers have been going down. A lot. But then I started getting really tired and the red blood count is low and that's why I'm tired. But no one said what's making it go low." He didn't comment. "So I got the transfusion. But it hardly did a thing. And I have no idea why and no one told me why. Now I'm getting pain. The patches work just fine but what's causing the pain?"

"Well, we're going to see Dr. Patel tomorrow. We can ask him then."

"No, I don't want to ask him. And I don't want you to ask him. I don't want to know any more than I do now. Things are starting to go bad and I'd just as soon not have the details. But . . . what's your take on all this, anyway?"

To my surprise he answered me frankly: "I have to admit that things don't look good. I don't know what's causing the pain but I think we have to face up to the fact that it might be caused by tumors. In spite of the tumor-marker numbers dropping. I don't know what else it could be. And if that's the case, tumors might be the cause of the red blood cell drop. And maybe the transfusion just isn't enough to overcome the negative effect of the tumors. I don't know."

"Are you worried?" I asked.

"Yes," he replied. Finally. "I'm worried. I'd like to ask him about it tomorrow. If it's ok with you."

"It's ok. I guess it's time. I want a straight answer."

Jack quizzed the doctor the next day. And I got my straight answer. It is like pulling teeth because Dr. Patel didn't like to give people bad news. In effect he said that in spite of the numbers going down the tumors were apparently growing. He would keep fighting, but when Jack pressed him, he admitted that he had no more weapons. As far as I was concerned, I was as good as dead.

A week later we went to Gilardi's Restaurant which I love and Jack hates. It was Rosum's birthday. My hands were shaking so badly I had to ask Jack to cut my food. This was a new one but it seemed that each week there was a new problem.

The next day there was a painful swelling in my left leg. The doctor gave me an anticoagulant called Heparin. Then a week later I started to get huge bruise marks on my legs and Jack called him. He said they were caused by the Heparin. He told Jack that it would be better if I got injections of something called Lovenox. The problem was that either Jack or I would have to give these injections to me daily and it should be given in the abdomen, away from the navel. Jack said he would do it and I was relieved. No way I wanted to do it. He got a video tape with the prescription, telling how to do injections. He did it every day at 5:00 P.M. Hurt like hell three days in a row. Then he called Nicole and told her what was happening. It's nice to have a daughter who's a nurse. She said to ignore the video tape and angle the needle about 45 degrees, instead of 90, and punch it in, instead if sliding it in. Worked like a charm, and I never felt a thing after that. Jack got quite good at it. Each time he did it I reminded him to stay away from the navel. It was our little joke, but this was one small way to try to be in charge of a life that is fast sliding beyond my control.

In the midst of these problems I went out with Rosum in the second week of March for our usual Saturday excursion. We went to have our nails done and then intended to go shopping. When we finished with the nails I was so exhausted I asked to go home. I didn't know it then, but it turned out to be our last Saturday outing.

On the 19*th* of March, the pain was starting to outrun the patches and Dr. Patel introduced us to a new thing. They were 'lollipops' made of a pain killer. Whenever I needed to supplement the patches, I could suck on one of these. They came in three strengths and two nurses from the drug company came to his office to tell me how to use them. They recommended that I start with the lowest dosage and work my way up if necessary. The lollipops were great and I loved having them.

I didn't tell Jack right away but by now the tumors were right there under the skin of my abdomen. I could feel them. It was only a matter of time before he found them too. When he gave me my shot one evening he stopped and started examining one of them. I told him I already knew about them. On occasion you could actually see the bumps.

I started to develop a terrific thirst and I needed everything I drank to be very cold. I always asked Jack to put lots of ice in my drinks. I loved lemonade the best. I had also developed awful constipation. Jack wanted me to take magnesium citrate, something you buy at the drugstore. It tasted horrible. He would put it in various things but nothing helped; I could still taste it. Nothing helped because I knew it was there. After a while I refused to take it. Later, I know he was sneaking it into my lemonade. But the constipation was so bad that I didn't mind the stuff anymore. To tell the truth, in lemonade it tastes pretty good.

Last week, on the 26*th* of March, we went to our niece Debbie's wedding. It was terrible for me and I felt like a zombie sitting there in my chair. I was too weak to do anything but sit there and even that took the utmost effort. I don't think I'll do another social outing. It's just not worth it.

The Lovenox worked well until the 4*th* of April when I developed a terrific pain in my left leg. Turns out it was a blood clot which formed in spite of the Lovenox. The doctor said that it just took some time for the Lovenox to work effectively. He gave me some Coumadin, a different coagulant. The pain, and presumably the clot, left.

I don't know when, but I can see the end is coming. I used to believe that I'd find some miracle that would cure everything. I don't believe that any more. Nothing is going to work.

I feel worst for Stephanie. I don't know what will become of her after I'm gone. Jack tries but it's not the same. He'll never take her shopping and he won't be as good as me to keep after Riverside and make sure they treat her right. Rosum will be wonderful as usual but it's not the same as her mother.

I don't feel as bad for Nicole. She's got Larry and in August she'll have the baby to take care of. Her life will be occupied but Stephanie's won't.

And I don't feel as bad for Jack. He's tough and he'll be able to carry on without me. Maybe someday he'll get married again, but I doubt it. Where would he find another one like me?

I've decided to stop writing. I have no more energy and I can't find it in me to keep going. I've enjoyed what I've written this far but now it's time to close up shop. I'll have to leave it to others to fill in the details of the rest of my life.

PROGRESSIVE RELAXATION & MEDITATION

Progressive Relaxation: This is a means of gradually relaxing your body and your mind. There are many forms of this. Here's one. Sit in a comfortable position or lie in bed just before going to sleep. Tell yourself that you are in a department store on the first floor. Everything on this first floor is white, the ceiling, the floor, the counters and pillars, and even the products on the counters. As you approach the escalator you can feel yourself starting to leave your stressful feelings behind and as you get on the escalator, look upward and notice that everything on the floor above you is a soothing shade of yellow. As you ride up this escalator you can already see the floor above coming into view. When you get off on this floor you look around at the ceiling, floors, counters and pillars, you note that they are all this relaxing shade of yellow. You can feel a calming light breeze washing over you all the time you are there.

You walk to the next Up escalator and as you get on it and look upward you see that the next floor contains a pale shade of blue. When you get off the escalator and look around, your relaxation deepens. You are not falling asleep but every muscle and nerve in your body feels like it is melting.

You get on the next Up escalator. With every floor you reach you find a soothing color of your choice that appeals to you and that relaxes you even more than the floor before.

Here's another. This combines the above color concept with a physical exercise.

Lie down and visualize all the parts of your body from your toes to your head. Color your toes and feet pale blur. Start by tightening the muscles in your toes then your feet. Hold this tightness while you color your calves and thighs a pale yellow. Tighten these also. By now your feet and the rest of your legs are remaining tight. Color your buttocks and abdomen light green. Tighten and hold these also. Color your arms and chest pink. Squeeze and keep them tight. Color your neck and face light gold. Tighten your neck and scrunch your face as if you had just experienced something unpleasant. Hold all this tightness to a count of 10.

Then start relaxing only one part and one color at a time. Start with your light gold face and neck. Relax them completely. Go to your pink arms and chest. Relax these, as you keep the lower part of your body tight. Continue this one part and one color at a time until you finally reach your toes and drain all the tension from them.

Feel how every part of your body now is totally relaxed. Lie where you are for at least a short while and enjoy the lack of stress.

Meditation: This is sometimes a strange word and strange concept to many of us. We probably tend to think of it as one of those ooey-gooey, *New Age* sort of things. It isn't. It is as ordinary as corn flakes. It can become part of your everyday life.

Here's what you do: find a comfortable sitting position (I don't recommend lying in bed; you might fall asleep). Start with your shoulders, which are where lots of your stress reside, and deliberately relax them. Then do a search of your body and try to identify muscles that are tight. Thighs? Back? Neck? Legs? Abdomen? If you can't relax them, don't worry about it. In a few minutes they will take care of themselves.

Start by breathing in and out slowly. You could use one of the mantras I mentioned earlier, at the end of Step 8.

Or you could simply count your breaths as you breathe out. Count to 10. Then start over and count to 10 again. Keep your eyes closed and your face relaxed. Do this for a few minutes at first then gradually work your way up to 20 minutes. This might take you a few weeks to achieve.

At first you will have a lot of thoughts coming into your mind. Let them. After you get good at this they will come in and then leave again. But don't try to push them out. For that matter don't *try* to do anything. Just let it be. Then allow yourself to return to your breaths or your mantra.

You might hear disturbing noises in the house or outside. Same thing. Let them be. Soon they will come in, but the difference is you will hear them but not process them.

Don't *try* to do anything. Just be present.

BOOKS CITED OR RECOMMENDED:

Siegel, Bernie *Love, Medicine & Miracles* (1990) Harper Paperbacks

Grollman, Earl *Living When A Loved One Has Died* (1997) Beacon Press

Kübler Ross, Elisabeth *On Death and Dying* (1997) Scribner Classics

Tolle, Eckhart *The Power of Now* (2004) New World Library

2685641

Made in the USA